TREASURE

TREASURE

Mike Groushko

SHOOTING STAR PRESS

A QUANTUM BOOK

Published by Shooting Star Press, Inc.
230 Fifth Avenue, Suite 1212
New York, NY 10001
USA

ISBN 1-57335-500-3

This book was produced by
Quantum Books Ltd
6 Blundell Street
London N7 9BH

Printed in China by Leefung-Asco Printers Ltd

CONTENTS

THE QUEST FOR TREASURE

"Where gold goes, blood flows!" is the lurid and folksy saying attributed to Mrs. Ova Noss, long-time watcher over one of America's legendary hidden treasures, the Apache gold of Victorio Peak in New Mexico, reputedly worth up to $300 billion.

The message is true enough. Many of the world's richest collections of valuables were amassed through bloodshed from before the time of the Assyrians, whose golden grave goods emerged in 1989 to amaze the most staid of experts. The trails to such splendors have often been tainted with gore, too. Nobody knows how many treasure seekers have died in their quests, either through natural hazards in inhospitable terrain or murdered for any of a dozen dark reasons.

For armchair lovers of real-life treasure yarns – and few of us are not – bloodshed past and perils present add spice to vicarious pleasure. The searchers in the field could almost certainly do without the danger, but brave it anyway. Some, on the other hand, revel in it.

There is no single stereotype of a treasure seeker. At one extreme are the bounty hunters motivated solely by greed, who dynamite old wrecks to get at the contents. At the other are the dedicated professional archaeologists, in whose scheme of things a seemingly ordinary potsherd may be of more significance than the most opulent item of gold.

Both feature in this book, along with countless others who fall somewhere in the middle range. But the beauty of the title "treasure-seeker" is that all can claim it, from the vacation beachcomber to the farmer contemplating the plowed earth as twilight falls. Some of their successes feature here, too. There is only one caveat: no responsible treasure seeker would trespass, steal, or risk damaging archaeological material. To do any or all is to sink to the level of the bounty hunter, and in most countries attract severe legal penalties.

Paradoxically, treasure seeking is becoming both easier and harder.

It is easier, first and foremost, because of developments in field technology. At the multimillion dollar end of the market are the computer-aided tracking devices and robots, such as those used in locating the wrecks of the Titanic *and the* Central America *in the 1980s. At the humbler end are metal detectors and scuba equipment, both of which have been widely available only for a relatively short time.*

Technical developments benefiting treasure seekers are not confined to the hunt itself. There are the improvements in communications, in health products (to protect against malaria and other infections), even in the library and archive services which have helped to direct many a treasure quest. To locate the Atocha, *a notable Florida treasure wreck, required months of work in Spanish archives; computerized and microfiche systems are cutting down the time such research takes.*

Treasure seeking is becoming harder because of the vast sums of money that could be involved, and because of the activities of the bounty hunters. Governments that once might have taken a relaxed view of properly organized searches on their territories are now much stricter; that has happened, for example, in Indonesia and on one of the reputedly richest of treasure islands, Cocos in the Pacific. Controls on export of valuables have been tightened up. Legal ownership battles can take years to resolve – even when the site is a mid-ocean shipwreck.

In many respects, these changes are for the better, but they have adverse effects. Truth becomes a casualty. The value of a potential treasure may be grossly inflated, to attract investors in the venture, or grossly underestimated to avoid the attentions of bounty hunters or legal claimants. Places and dates of finds are sometimes fictionalized or concealed altogether. Because of the rising stakes, the ruthlessness of some bounty hunters has re-emerged, to the point where respectable archaeologists on authorized digs need permanent armed guards even in supposedly civilized parts of the world.

None of this mars the romantic allure of hidden treasure. In the comfort of an armchair, all can dream. And who knows what awaits on the next walk along the beach, through the woods, or in the park.

1: TREASURE ISLANDS

Thanks to Robert Louis Stevenson's 1883 novel Treasure Island, *few islands anywhere in the world – and even fewer in the Caribbean Sea and the Indian Ocean – are without their stories of hidden pirate gold. Stevenson, though, based his fiction on fact. The pirates and privateers of the old Spanish Main and elsewhere did stash their spoils where they hoped no one else could find them.*

Sometimes, these riches come to light, as they are doing at the old buccaneer capital of Port Royal, Jamaica, and are said to have done on Cocos Island in the Pacific.

These occasional finds keep an army of treasure hunters going, searching for the island hoards of the likes of Henry Morgan, William Kidd, and – perhaps biggest and best of all – William Thompson, the opportunist who made off with the choicest valuables in the whole golden city of Lima.

THE SPANISH MAIN

*I*n the three centuries after Columbus's first voyage to the New World on behalf of Spain, the Spanish systematically stripped their American colonies of vast wealth in gold, silver, and gems. The process of plunder reached its height between about 1550 and 1650, when three fleets a year of treasure-heavy galleons, escorted by fighting ships, brought the colonial spoils across the ocean to Spain.

Once in the open Atlantic, the Spanish convoys, or plate fleets, were relatively safe. But on putting out from their bases in Central and South America, these floating treasuries had first to navigate the treacherous waters between the islands of the Caribbean, where they were at the mercy of hurricanes, reefs – and sea raiders. For the lure of Spanish ships, each laden with millions of dollars' worth of precious items, brought desperadoes from France, England, Holland, and elsewhere to prey on them, and on the strongholds where their cargoes were assembled.

Sometimes, these raiders were licensed by states officially at war with Spain, when they were termed privateers or, in the Caribbean, buccaneers, from a French word for the smoked meat that was part of their shipboard diet. The privateers were supposed to hand over most of the

BELOW Edward 'Blackbeard' Teach, here in combat with a Moorish prince, reveled in his reputation for cruelty. His booty is said still to lie in an unlocated underground hideaway.

Black Beard.   Abdellah the Prince.

ABOVE *Welsh-born Henry Morgan led the notorious privateers of Port Royal, Jamaica, around 1670. The vast loot he captured from the Spanish stronghold of Panama City remains untraced.*

Terre and Grande Ile, Barataria Bay, Louisiana. In the Caribbean, they stretch from the Bahamas in the west to Barbados in the east, through such notorious pirate bases as Tortuga (Ile Tortue) off Haiti and the Isle of Pines off Cuba.

Pirates may have had an incentive to hide their hauls, to protect them from other pirates or the authorities. Privateers gone bad certainly had one. If they revealed the existence of booty taken from the enemy, they were obliged to share it with the authorities; if the booty came from friendly or neutral sources, the takers faced the death penalty as pirates. That is why the most convincing tales of hidden treasure are associated with privateers such as Morgan and Kidd, rather than with out-and-out sea criminals like Edward "Blackbeard" Teach. Whether hidden by privateers or pirates, few of the Caribbean's reputed treasure caches are known to have been found. Clues to the whereabouts of some of them may now be emerging in Port Royal, Jamaica.

plunder to the licensing power, and not to attack friendly or neutral ships. Many ignored these restrictions if a prize presented itself, becoming no better than the freebooting pirates who owed allegiance to none, and who were also drawn by the rich Caribbean pickings.

Among the first of the buccaneers were Frenchmen such as François "Pegleg" le Clerc and Jacques de Sores, ransacker of Havana in 1555. Among the last were the American Jean Lafitte and the renegade Spaniard José Gaspar, known as "Gasparilla," or "Richard Coeur de Lion," sunk with his captured treasure in the Gulf of Mexico by the U.S. Navy in 1821. Between them came many whose names are legend – John "Long Ben" Avery, John "Calico Jack" Rackham, the female pirate Anne Bonny, Henry Morgan, and William Kidd.

Their crimes and exploits gave us our image of pirates, and of treasure islands. For there is hardly an island of the thousands in the Gulf of Mexico and the Caribbean without its tale of stolen gold, buried and never reclaimed. In the Gulf, they include Gasparilla's hideaway near Charlotte Harbor, Florida, and Lafitte's Grande

BELOW *The romantic view of piracy reached its peak in the 19th century, thanks to illustrations such as this one of sea-rovers burying their spoils in an island cave.*

"THE WICKEDEST CITY ON EARTH"

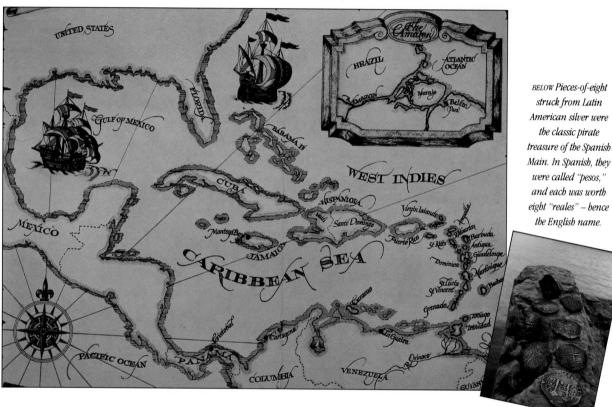

RIGHT The Caribbean Sea and adjoining waters of the 'Spanish Main' are probably the site of more hidden or lost treasures than anywhere else on earth. For more than three centuries, they were the hunting ground of freebooters from all nations.

BELOW Pieces-of-eight struck from Latin American silver were the classic pirate treasure of the Spanish Main. In Spanish, they were called "pesos," and each was worth eight "reales" – hence the English name.

When at 20 minutes to noon on June 7, 1692, an earthquake and tidal wave tipped Port Royal in Jamaica into the Caribbean, pious local inhabitants claimed the disaster was a punishment from God. Since Port Royal had been developed by the English four decades earlier, it had become what a contemporary visitor called "the wickedest city on earth," notorious for its brothels, gambling dens, and taverns, and the licentiousness of many of its 6,500 citizens. Two-thirds of them perished in the quake and the plague that followed it.

Port Royal was also stunningly wealthy – the richest English-speaking settlement in the western hemisphere, and with a per-capita income nearly equal to that of the City of London at the time. The foundations of its fortune and unsavory reputation were laid by buccaneers.

Between 1655 and 1660, an English expeditionary force had wrested Jamaica from the Spanish. But the English did not then have a permanent fleet in the Caribbean, and without sea protection it was feared the island could be recaptured by Spain, or taken by the French or Dutch. The solution was for the English governor to turn Jamaica in general, and Port Royal in particular, into a haven for privateers.

Freebooters from all over the Caribbean, and of all nationalities, flocked to this licensed sanctuary. They elected an "admiral" to lead them – initially, a Dutchman called Edward Mansveldt or Mansfield. With a fleet of 15 vessels, 500 men, and an able second-in-command in the

notorious Henry Morgan, Mansfield plundered Spanish settlements in Cuba and central America, returning with a huge booty to Jamaica. Much of the proceeds of these and other raids went on wild living; it was not unknown for a seaman to get through thousands of dollars in one night's carousing in Port Royal.

When the earthquake struck, Port Royal was already settling into calmer ways. The privateers' licenses to loot were revoked in 1670-71, but the town remained a magnet for disreputable seafarers, and a treasure store for ill-gotten gains.

Much of the portable wealth of Port Royal may have been removed by native divers soon after the disaster. But underwater excavations since the late 1950s have revealed much more, including a cache of silver pieces-of-eight, silver plate, huge assemblies of 17th-century pewter items and bottles, ships' cannon, and many other priceless artifacts, both everyday and rare. The remains of entire buildings have also been preserved under the silt, enabling experts from Texas A&M University's Institute of Nautical Archaelogy to build up a picture of life in the "wickedest city."

ABOVE The palm-fringed beaches and rocky outcrops of the Caribbean islands once bore witness to bloody battles between treasure-hungry freebooters and the guardians of Spanish riches.

RIGHT Underwater excavations at the buccaneers' capital of Port Royal have yielded vast quantities of pewter jugs, plates, and spoons, dating from before the destructive earthquake of 1692.

MORGAN: MOST SUCCESSFUL PIRATE

RIGHT Henry Morgan (?1635–1688), sailor-of-fortune and suspected pirate, rose to become lieutenant-governor of Jamaica and a scourge of the Caribbean buccaneers.

Sᵣ HEN: MORGAN

*I*n the mid-1960s, the American marine archaeologist Robert Marx, working for the Jamaican government, made one of his most notable finds at Port Royal. It was a treasure chest bearing the crest of the Spanish king and stuffed with hundreds of silver coins, many of them freshly minted at the silver centers of Potosi (Colombia) and Lima (Peru). The wooden chest itself crumbled almost immediately, leaving only the brass lock. But could the find be a clue to an enduring riddle of the Caribbean and a central figure in it – Henry Morgan?

Morgan, a Welshman born in about 1635, came to prominence as a member of the English force that took Jamaica from the Spanish. He later became second-in-command to Edward Mansfield among the Port Royal privateers. After Mansfield died during a visit to the French pirates' base on Tortuga Island off Haiti, Morgan event-

ually took over as the privateers' "admiral." However, he was suspected of failing to share the spoils of his daring raids against the Spanish with the English government that licensed him, and in 1672 he was shipped back to England to be tried for piracy. Such was Morgan's popular appeal, though, that he escaped the gallows, received a knighthood from King Charles II, and returned to Jamaica as lieutenant-governor. He amassed huge wealth and estates, and died of alcoholism in 1688.

In 1670, during his privateering heyday, Morgan assembled a fleet of 36 ships and some 2,000 men at Port Royal for a raid

BELOW Morgan and his men attack the Spanish stronghold of Puerto del Principe on Cuba in 1668. The illustration comes from a famous early study of piracy – Oexmelin's "Histoire des Boucaniers d'Amérique," published in 1699.

The Towne of Puerto del Principe taken & sackt

on Panama City, then the richest center in the whole of the New World. To reach it, he sailed across the Caribbean to the Chagres River, and marched through the thick jungle of the Panama Isthmus to the Pacific coast. Outmaneuvered by Morgan, the Spanish defenders of Panama City fled, putting it to the torch.

Morgan spent several weeks in Panama, searching for spoils and torturing captives for information. Then he loaded gold and silver coins (including 750,000 pieces-of-eight, according to some sources), plate, and jewelry onto a train of more than 100 mules and returned across the isthmus to his ships. His men received a meager share of about $1,500 each at today's values, while Morgan's vessel quietly slipped anchor, bound for no one knows where. Morgan's fellow-captains, and the English authorities, believed he had filched the best part of the plunder for himself, concealing it somewhere between Panama and Jamaica. For that, he was arrested on suspicion of piracy when he eventually turned up at Port Royal.

Restored to respectability by King Charles, Morgan made no reference to hidden treasure during the rest of his life, though some of his crew did. The mystery of the missing loot of Panama remains. Perhaps it will be solved in the Port Royal excavations.

ABOVE and BELOW The Spanish treasure-city of Portobelo, on the Panamanian isthmus, successfully held out against Morgan in 1665. But within three years he was back there, taking booty that included 250,000 pieces-of-eight. Though he eventually became a knight, Morgan was no gentleman. He threatened and tortured his prisoners until they revealed the whereabouts of their valuables.

KIDD: PLEA-BARGAIN
BEFORE THE GALLOWS

Privateering brought the drunken and cruel Henry Morgan wealth, position, and respectability. To his near-contemporary William Kidd (1645?-1701), a well-regarded naval officer turned merchant and flower of New York society, it brought ignominy and death. It also brought the greater fame – or notoriety.

LEFT *The agreement that brought William Kidd to the gallows for piracy was signed in October 1695, with the Governor of New York, Lord Bellomont, and Robert Livingston. It was Livingston who initiated the whole fateful deal.*

Kidd's adventures as a privateer in the service of New York's Governor the Earl of Bellomont and his highly publicized trial made him the prototype figure for dozens of "Treasure Island" style pirate yarns. On the eve of his execution he attempted to buy his life by offering to reveal the whereabouts of a treasure cache said to be worth $200,000 at 1701 prices. The discovery in England, more than 200 years later, of four cryptic maps attributed to Kidd, unleashed countless treasure hunts along the East Coast of North America, in the Indian Ocean, and as far afield as Japan. They continue today.

The seeds of Kidd's downfall were sown in 1695, when he agreed with Governor Lord Bellomont to command a private operation against pirates plaguing English shipping in the Atlantic and Indian Oceans. Any spoils were to be divided between the pair, with Bellomont getting 60 percent. What Kidd did not know was that Bellomont had various powerful backers in England, including King William III.

The expedition was a disaster. Kidd's ship, the *Adventure Galley*, failed to take any worthwhile prizes in a year of cruising. The crew, who saw little distinction between pirate vessels and other laden craft, became increasingly mutinous over the lack of spoils. Eventually, in seeming desperation, Kidd started attacking any ship or seaboard settlement that presented the opportunity. One victim was the *Quedah Merchant*, an Armenian vessel with an English captain. That was too much for the English Admiralty, which declared Kidd a pirate.

Kidd, who had sailed to the freebooters' nest of Ile Ste. Marie, Madagascar, to divide

LEFT and BELOW Deserted by his powerful backers, Kidd was left to stand trial alone, in a hearing that caused a public sensation. Kidd's attempt to buy his life started one of the world's most enduring treasure quests.

the spoils and change ships from the leaky *Adventure Galley* to the *Quedah Merchant*, learned the news on reaching the West Indies on his voyage home. Nevertheless, he continued along the American coast in another ship, the *Antonio*, eventually to land at Boston. He evidently thought his patron Bellomont would protect him from the piracy charge. But Bellomont had him arrested and transferred to England.

When Kidd finally went on trial before the House of Commons in London, Bellomont was dead and some of his backers in Kidd's expedition, including the First Lord of the Admiralty, had been arraigned for their role in the affair. In the atmosphere of public scandal, Kidd was left to carry the blame, found guilty, and sentenced to hang at Execution Dock. His attempt to buy his life with the promise of hidden riches counted for nothing with the Speaker of the House of Commons. Kidd went to his death on May 23, 1701 – leaving a legacy of treasure island tales to grow.

MYSTERIES OF THE MAPS

hether William Kidd did actually hide some of his spoils from privateering and piracy has puzzled treasure hunters for more than 250 years. The only real evidence for such a cache is Kidd's eve-of-execution letter to the Speaker of the House of Commons, which states: "In my proceedings in the Indies, I have lodged goods and Tresure to the value of £100,000...." The mention of the Indies is hardly a clue, since it refers to the whole voyage, not to a treasure site.

BELOW Theories abound over the resting place of Kidd's treasure – if it existed at all. Sites in the Caribbean, the western Atlantic, and the Indian Ocean have all been suggested for his mysterious island.

KIDD IN THE EAST?

In 1952, a party of Japanese fishermen were forced by rough weather to take shelter on the tiny island of Yokoate, one of a chain stretching from Japan southwest to Taiwan. They found strange carvings on rocks half-hidden in deep undergrowth. The carvings seemed to represent horned animals.

Back in Japan, the fishermen boasted of their adventures and their finds. A leading scholar, Nagashima, made a dramatic connection. He recalled that Kidd sometimes used a visual play on his surname instead of a signature; the drawing was of a young goat with horns. Could the Yokoate carvings be kids – and Kidd's?

Nagashima is known to have gone to Yokoate to investigate, but after that, rumor takes over. The Japanese scholar is reputed to have found, near the carvings, a cave. Inside, allegedly, were a number of old iron chests brimming with gold and silver coins, worth perhaps at least some $60 million or more. These Nagashima supposedly had secretly shipped back to Japan, after which he, and they, disappeared.

If the tale is true it would mean that the China Sea reference on treasure charts attributed to Kidd is reasonably accurate, not a deliberate attempt to mislead. The question remains, however, of whether Kidd ever really visited the area, and, if he did, when.

Alternatively, the maps may have come from a previous voyage of Kidd's, or were not originally Kidd's at all, but captured and copied by Kidd.

Yet another possibility is that the maps may be fakes – though that does not necessarily discredit the story in Kidd's original letter. Of course, that letter itself could have been a bluff, the lie of a man desperate to buy his life.

What is certain is that one portion of Kidd's treasure was found long ago, on Gardiner's Island, near the entrance to Long Island Sound. Sometime in 1699, before landing in Boston, Kidd offloaded bales and chests there, including some containing gold. Rumors of the cache may well have reached Kidd's patron Bellomont, who, sensing a swindle, withdrew his protection. In any case, Bellomont was quick to collect the items once Kidd was arrested.

ABOVE One site where Kidd is known to have buried some of his treasure is Gardiner's Island, near New York. The booty was quickly located by agents of the Earl of Bellomont in 1699.

Between 1929 and 1935, an English former lawyer called Hubert Palmer turned up no fewer than four maps purporting to show Kidd's treasure island. Each was found hidden in a chest or desk of about the right age, bearing Kidd's name. In each, the writing resembles known examples of Kidd's. The most detailed map clearly places it in the China Sea, which Kidd is not likely to have visited on his last, ill-starred voyage of 1696-99.

Various explanations are possible. One is that the maps have been made deliberately misleading. The "China Sea" could in reality be the Caribbean, where Kidd abandoned the *Quedah Merchant*; it could be the Atlantic coast of North America, where Kidd put in several times before reaching Boston.

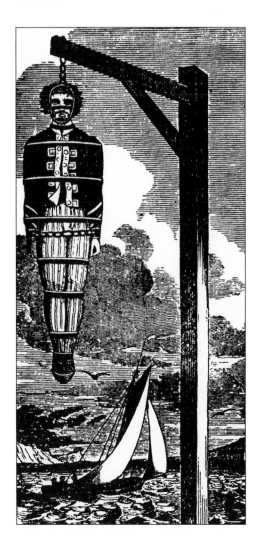

LEFT The bodies of pirates hanged for their crimes were left to rot on dockside gibbets in 18th-century London, as a deterrent to other seamen who might be tempted to copy their exploits.

OAK ISLAND'S MONEY PIT

A teen-age boy by the name of Daniel McGinnis unwittingly launched one of the world's longest-running quests for hidden treasure when, in 1795, he and two friends began digging in a saucer-shaped hollow they had found on Oak Island, four miles off the Nova Scotia coast in Canada. For the hollow marked the entrance to what has been called the *Money Pit*, a possible cache of pirate gold linked by some to William Kidd's mysterious hoard.

Over the past two centuries, millions of dollars and several lives have been lost in trying to fathom the pit's secrets. But by 1989 it had still not yielded them in full.

The pit itself is an extremely complicated structure which modern engineers reckon would have taken 20 people two years to create. It is based on a natural blowhole or shaft descending more than 200 feet at the eastern end of Oak Island to a large and otherwise inaccessible cave. At intervals down the shaft, the builders placed 10 or so wooden platforms to block it. Two side tunnels connected the main shaft with the sea, in such a way that, as certain platforms were removed, the shaft would flood, thus protecting whatever lies below.

Daniel McGinnis and a group of fellow searchers sprang this water trap in 1803, when they were several platforms and 98 feet down into the shaft. Since then, the flooded pit has defied many efforts to reach the bottom. In the 1970s, the Triton salvage company used modern equipment to probe the shaft and cave to a depth of 212 feet. Their underwater cameras are said to have revealed what could be three sea chests, protected by a severed human

hand. But even now, nearly two decades later, the pit is still a mystery.

Items so far recovered at Oak Island only add to the puzzle of who built the Money Pit, when, and why. They include a stone marked with the date 1704, the remains of an iron chain, and iron scissors that may have been made in Mexico. The dated stone seems to rule out William Kidd, who was hanged for piracy in 1701. On the other hand, the island in the treasure maps that appeared this century and that have been attributed to Kidd looks very much like Oak; one even has what seems to be the word "oak" concealed in it.

Another suggested builder of the Money Pit is Edward "Blackbeard" Teach, the Bahamas-based pirate who operated off the American East Coast until 1718. He boasted of an underground store hiding his booty "where none but Satan and myself can find it."

But local records at Chester, over the bay from Oak, hint that the pit may have been constructed later still. In 1763, Chester residents saw strange lights and fires on the island. Perhaps wisely, they did not investigate, and it was left to young Daniel McGinnis, 32 years later, to open the Oak Island treasure trail.

LEFT Wooded Oak Island, off Canada's Atlantic coast, bears a marked resemblance to the island shown in treasure maps that purportedly once belonged to Captain Kidd.

RIGHT For nearly 200 years, the mysterious Money Pit at the eastern end of Oak Island has defied strenuous efforts by treasure-seekers to lay bare its secrets.

SEEKING CAPTAIN KIDD'S TREASURE OAK ISLAND CHESTER N.S.

DANGER KEEP OUT
PARTS OF THIS AREA
MAY CAVE IN

THE MONEY PIT
TREASURE SEEKERS HAVE FOUND:
EVERY 10 FEET A PLATFORM OF LOGS
40 FEET A TIER OF CHARCOAL
50 FEET STONES WITH NUMBERS
60 FEET MANILLA GRASS
70 FEET RIND OF COCONUT
80 FEET TIER OF PUTTY
93 FEET THE WARNING STONE

RICHES OF COCOS

BELOW Dividing the booty.

A 2-foot-high gold statue of the Madonna recovered from the sea at Cocos Island (Ile del Coco) off Costa Rica in 1931 bears mute witness to three centuries of Pacific Ocean piracy – and perhaps the richest treasure island of them all. For while most freebooters seeking Spanish gold and silver preferred to lurk in the Caribbean, with its myriad hideaways, some operated on the western edge of Spain's American possessions. Hot and humid Cocos Island, 400 miles out into the ocean, was used by many Pacific raiders, and is associated with at least three known hoards. Treasure seekers who have visited it with varying degrees of success include the young Franklin D. Roosevelt; but like many others he found nothing.

The tradition of Pacific attacks on Spanish wealth stretches back to the 16th century and Sir Francis Drake, hero to the English, bloodthirsty pirate to the Spaniards. One of Drake's greatest coups during a career in which he captured more than 100 Spanish ships occurred in the Pacific off Ecuador, with the taking in 1579 of the *Cacafuego*. She carried 26 tons of silver, 80 pounds of gold, and a dozen chests of coins, as well as secret charts indicating a treasure hoard on the isthmus of Panama which has not been traced to this day.

Some 100 years after Drake, another English sea captain, William Davis, made

RIGHT Buccaneers fight a duel over who is to get the treasure in this early 20th-century painting by Howard Pyle. Many of Pyle's illustrations of pirates first appeared in Harper's Magazine *in the 1900s.*

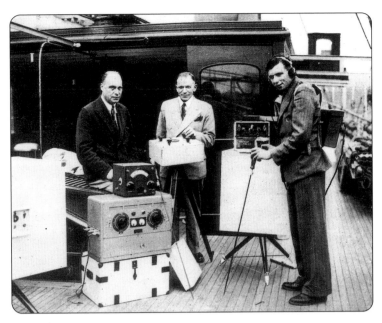

ABOVE Members of a British expedition of 1934 to Cocos Island display some of the scientific apparatus, including an early metal detector, they intended to use to seek out reputed treasure-hoards.

BELOW The 1934 treasure hunt on Cocos came to an ignominious end, when Costa Rican police ordered the hunters to leave the island. The search for the pirate gold of Cocos continues . . .

Cocos a base from which to prey on the Spanish. He planned to top Drake's feats by capturing an entire Spanish treasure-fleet putting out from Lima in Peru. But to do so, Davis allied himself with a French naval force. When it came to the action, the French stood off, and Davis was defeated. Nevertheless, Davies accumulated ample booty during his life of piracy, which ended when he disappeared mysteriously in 1702. Some of this plunder is said still to be on Cocos.

Davis was eventually succeeded on Cocos by Benito Bonito, a shadowy figure variously thought to be Portuguese, English, or a renegade Spaniard. Using the island as his headquarters, Bonito in 1819 raided the Mexican coast near Acapulco, capturing a large cargo of Spanish gold which he hid at Wafer Bay, Cocos. A year or so later, Bonito died – killed in action, or hanged, depending on the source – before he could reclaim his cache.

But he left maps of its whereabouts with a woman who claimed to have been his mistress, and with a member of his crew. In the 1880s, the maps came into the hands of a German seaman, August Gissler, who spent 20 years on Cocos hunting for the hoard. All he turned up were a few old coins, and he died in poverty in New York in 1930.

Within two years of Gissler's death, treasure seekers using the newly invented metal detector announced they had found a store of gold precisely where Bonito's maps showed it would be. Some now doubt this claim, but there is no doubt about the gold Madonna, retrieved by the Belgian Peter Bergmans and sold by him in New York for $11,000. That came to light, not at Bonito's Wafer Bay, but elsewhere on the coast. It could be a signpost on the trail to the biggest Cocos cache of all, believed to include another Madonna fashioned in pure gold – this one life-sized!

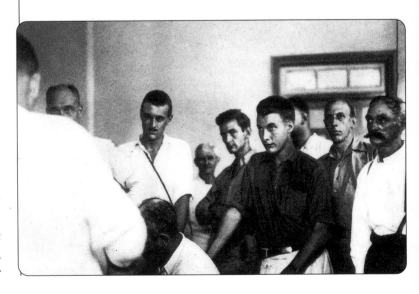

OUR LADY OF LIMA

By the 1820s, Spain's American empire was collapsing in the face of internal strife. The rebel army of Simón Bolívar was threatening Lima in Peru, among the richest of the Spanish settlements. Desperate to escape, the wealthiest citizens sought a ship to carry them and many of Lima's valuables to Panama City. The only suitable vessel available was the brig *Mary Dear*, captained by a Scotsman, William Thompson.

Thompson loaded the treasure – including a jewel-bedecked golden Madonna weighing more than a ton, reliquaries, gems, and coins – and set sail. The fate of the passengers is not known, but the *Mary Dear* made for Cocos Island. Once there, Thompson shared out some of the prize with his crew and hid the rest in or near a cave.

Unfortunately for the Scotsman, the Spaniards were watching his movements. They boarded the *Mary Dear* after it had left Cocos and put most of the crew to death for theft. Thompson and his first mate were spared to guide the Spaniards back to the treasure cave, but once on Cocos the two escaped. The Spaniards left empty-handed, and the pair were later rescued by a passing whaler.

The mate died soon afterward. Thompson lived for some years, but could not get back to Cocos. Just before his death, he gave a map pinpointing the treasure to John Keating, a seafaring friend. Keating mounted at least one expedition to Cocos in the 1840s, found Thompson's cave, and removed what he could carry in his pockets. However, Keating's crew mutinied and he, too, was forced to hide until rescued. The treasure retrieved from the island was enough to set Keating up as a businessman and farmer in Newfoundland, but much more remained.

Since Keating's foray, countless fortune-hunters have gone to Cocos Island looking for the Lima gold. Landmarks corresponding to those mentioned by Keating and Thompson have been identified near Chatham Bay, though no treasure was traced near them. Two people claimed to have seen at least part of the gold, but for obscure reasons did not remove it. One, in 1875, was a seaman called Bob Flower. The other was the Belgian Peter Bergmans who, in 1931, maintained he had found a cave containing chests and a human skeleton, but refused to lead anyone back to it.

In 1966, four young Frenchmen conducted a clandestine search on the island. In a hillside cave near Chatham Bay they say they stumbled on a macabre scene – the skeletons of two men who had evidently killed each other. Beside the pair were pickaxes, camping gear, and several wooden chests. In two of the chests, in equal quantities, were Spanish gold coins and gold bars, which the Frenchmen are said subsequently to have smuggled off Cocos. Other items found, including a Bible, suggest the pair must have arrived on the island after 1840, so they could not have been members of Thompson's original crew, but were early questers after the golden Madonna of Lima.

RIGHT Wafer Bay on Cocos Island was used as a base by pirates William Davis and Benito Bonito. It has yielded some treasure, and may yet produce more. But the most magnificent Cocos prize of all – hidden there by William Thompson and including the lifesized golden Madonna of Lima – is said to lie around the headland, somewhere near Chatham Bay.

PIRATE KINGS
OF MADAGASCAR

By the end of the 18th century, the destruction of their haven at Port Royal and increased patrols by the English and French navies had made the Caribbean too hot for many of its buccaneers. They shifted their sphere of operations across the Atlantic and around the Cape of Good Hope, to the Indian Ocean. There, the pickings were both rich and easy – merchantmen of Portugal, Holland, and England returning to Europe laden with the treasures of the East.

The incomers found stiff competition from local pirates who practiced their cruel trade along the coasts of India, around the Persian Gulf, and in the islands of Indonesia. But Madagascar, at the western end of the Indian Ocean, provided a safe base where European buccaneers could live like kings. Several cut-throats installed themselves as petty monarchs over Madagascan tribes, among them James Plantain, whose "kingdom" and treasure store was at Ranter Bay, and a Frenchman called Misson, who founded a piratical "commune" at Diego Suarez Bay. Misson's native communards eventually rose up against him, forcing him to flee, but only after he had buried the vast booty he had amassed. It has never been traced.

The greatest pirates' center on Madagascar, however, was the infamous Ile Ste. Marie, halfway down the eastern coast. Among the buccaneers to use it was the Englishman John Avery, nicknamed "Long Ben" and made famous by Charles Johnson's play *The Successful Pirate*, staged at Drury Lane, London in 1695. Avery's coups between 1691 and 1696 included the capture of a ship, the

RIGHT At the end of the 17th century "Long Ben" Avery was the most famous pirate of them all, thanks to his capture of a treasure-ship belonging to an Indian mogul, or prince. Its cargo included a fortune in gold, silver, and diamonds.

Gunsway, belonging to an Indian prince, from which he and his companions are said to have taken 200,000 gold and silver coins and a large quantity of diamonds. Avery swindled his partners out of their share and set off on a circuitous voyage from Madagascar to the Bahamas to Boston, Massachusetts, and eventually to Ireland and England. Ironically, Avery himself is reputed to have been swindled out of the proceeds of the diamonds and gold items he entrusted to English merchants to sell, and to have died a pauper in his native Devon. The fate of the coins is not clear, but many were lost when Avery was shipwrecked outside Nassau harbor in the Bahamas and remain untraced.

It was to the Ile Ste. Marie that William Kidd came in 1698, on the voyage that brought him to the gallows. Nothing could have been more damning to Kidd, hired to fight pirates, than his unhindered departure from this pirates' nest.

The Ile Ste. Marie is a possible site, too, for a lost pirate treasure as famous and as romantically puzzling as that of Kidd – the multimillion dollars' worth of spoils amassed by the Frenchman Olivier Le

Vasseur, known as "La Buse," or "The Buzzard." On his own and with various associates, including the Englishmen John Taylor and Edward England and fellow-Frenchman Bernadin Nageon de l'Estang (nicknamed "Butin," or "Plunder"), Le Vasseur terrorized the Indian Ocean between 1720 and 1730. As well as the Ile Ste. Marie, Le Vasseur at various times based himself on the islands of Mauritius and Réunion (on both of which Nageon is said to have stashed treasure) – and, it is thought, at Mahé in the Seychelles. A hunt for Le Vasseur's hoard has been going on at Mahé for nearly 70 years.

BELOW A shipwreck and double-dealing by merchants to whom he entrusted his stolen gold and diamonds left Long Ben – the "Successful Pirate" – a pauper in the autumn of his life.

THE BUZZARD'S TRAIL

'Find my treasure he who can!" cried Olivier Le Vasseur just before he was hanged for piracy on the French island of Réunion on July 7, 1730. With these words, he flung into the watching crowd a piece of paper bearing a series of cryptic symbols.

It was a challenge worth pursuing – for in his 10-year career of theft and violence in the Indian Ocean, Le Vasseur, "the Buzzard," had accumulated spoils whose present-day value is estimated at more than $500 million. His greatest prize was the *Virgen del Cabo* (*La Vierge du Cap*), a treasure ship belonging to the Bishop of Goa, the Portuguese colony in India. Le Vasseur and his then partner, the English pirate John Taylor, found in the vessel's hold "rivers of diamonds, a large quantity of gold bars, cascades of gold coins, and cases and chests of sacred church vessels." Among all this wealth was the diamond-encrusted, golden Fiery Cross of Goa, an opulent crucifix which, it is said, required three men to lift.

BELOW Wreckage from a Portuguese ship lost in Seychelles waters.

Le Vasseur hid his share of this booty somewhere in the islands of the Indian Ocean and apparently tried to lead a respectable life, even returning some of the treasure through an intermediary. He was offered an amnesty by the French authorities, but when he realized that would mean giving up the rest of his ill-gotten fortune, turned them down, and eventually resumed his raiding. Ship-wrecked off Madagascar, the Buzzard was trapped by the French, tried, and sentenced to death. The coded paper he flung from the scaffold was drawn up while he awaited execution.

BELOW Nails, buckles and other 18th-century artifacts found near Bel Ombre Bay on Mahé.

28

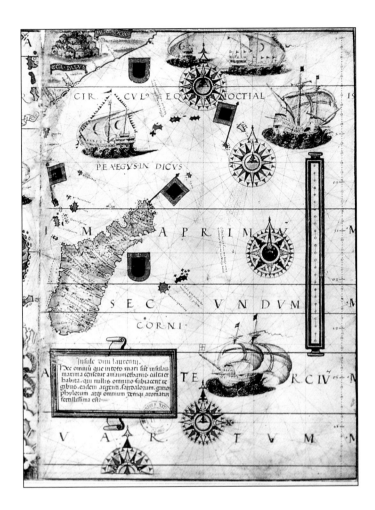

A document thought to be the Buzzard's cryptogram came to light in the Seychelles, 1,100 miles north of Réunion, shortly after the First World War. In 1948, it was acquired by a former British army officer, Reginald Cruise-Wilkins, who believed it indicated Le Vasseur's cache was at Bel Ombre Bay on Mahé, the main island of the Seychelles group.

Cruise-Wilkins spent the rest of his life searching around Bel Ombre, finding dozens of 18th-century non-precious artifacts and even what appeared to be a pirates' graveyard of the same period. These, it is claimed, suggest Le Vasseur and a band of up to 250 men may have spent considerable time in the area between 1725 and 1729, when little is recorded of the Buzzard's activities.

Reginald Cruise-Wilkins died in 1977, asserting he was only six or so yards from the treasure. In 1988, his son John resumed the quest, inspired by reports of a metal object the size of a table traced by remote survey in Bel Ombre Bay. But by the end of 1989 no results of this search had been publicly announced.

Bel Ombre's notable features include a strange series of rock carvings and stone sculptures, depicting birds, snakes, a human nose, and female genitalia. According to Reginald Cruise-Wilkins, these link up with the Buzzard's cryptogram and relate in some way to the mythological Labors of Hercules. Others who have studied the Le Vasseur document maintain either that it is indecipherable or that, when deciphered, it is gibberish.

LEFT The granite islands of the Seychelles, first mapped in 1501, remained uninhabited until France claimed them in the mid-18th century. Before annexation, they were a safe haven for Indian Ocean pirates. Legends of hidden treasure abound.

BELOW The turquoise waters and silvery beaches of the Seychelles once rang to the raucous shouts of European pirates, who reputedly brought female captives to the islands for debauchery. Seychellais fishermen are a rich source of folklore about the island's hidden treasures.

The coded message, thrown into the crowd by the Buzzard before being hanged, could reveal where his treasures are buried (©Bibliothèque Nationale, Reunion).

2 : UNDER
THE WAVES

Modern technology makes it possible to find and lift magnificent treasures from undersea wrecks that may have lain undisturbed for centuries, untouched capsules of their times.

Since 1945, salvors have raised enough gold, silver, and jewels to ransom a multitude of kings. It comes from old ships such as Spanish plate galleons and Portuguese East Indiamen. It comes, too, from more modern vessels like the Edinburgh, *with its $70 million in Russian bullion, and the* Central America, *with perhaps a staggering $1 billion in California gold.*

But gold and gems are not everything. Archaeologists and historians drool over their own sea-bed treasures – everyday objects shedding light on the past, such as those from a 3,500-year-old wreck off Turkey. No price can be put on them.

The quest is becoming more intense, with many known huge prizes still to go for. The biggest of all, experts judge, lies off Indonesia. That could yield treasure worth up to $9 billion.

THE OLDEST WRECK

RIGHT Artifacts raised from ancient shipwrecks off Turkey are priceless to archaeologists for what they reveal of Mediterranean life centuries before the time of Christ.

rich store of artifacts and raw materials originating from no fewer than seven civilizations that flourished in and around the eastern Mediterranean in the Late Bronze Age. The varied sources of supply of the cargo shows how complex Mediterranean trade patterns were three millennia ago – though it seems likely that only a powerful ruler would have had the authority and resources to assemble the items, and that such shiploads were rare.

'*I*'ve never seen gold like that under water...never, ever!" exclaimed Robin Piercy from Texas's Institute of Nautical Archaeology as he surfaced from a dive onto the world's oldest known shipwreck. The vessel, a 50-foot trading craft probably dating from the 14th century BC, was found by a sponge diver in 1982 in 150 feet of water off Ulu Burun, on Turkey's Mediterranean coast.

By treasure hunters' standards, the item that occasioned Piercy's excitement was relatively modest. It was a plain gold chalice made from two metal cones simply riveted together. Astonishingly, it still glittered after perhaps 3,500 years in the sea.

To archaeologists, the Ulu Burun ship is one of the most important finds of all time. From it, they have now recovered a

LEFT A diver takes a basket of artifacts up to a submerged decompression chamber.

RIGHT *Ten U.S.
millionaires were
among the 1,513 people
who died in the
"Titanic" disaster of
1912. The wealth of so
many of the liner's
passengers fed
rumours that the
wreck, relocated in
1985, holds a fortune
in jewelry.*

Pottery from Mycenae in Greece, from Cyprus and from Egypt was found by the excavators alongside huge wine jars from the Canaanite civilization in what are now present-day Israel and Syria. Canaan was probably the source, too, of a magnificent gold falcon pendant and silver bracelets; another gold pendant, of a naked goddess, may have come from further north, on the edge of the Hittite empire in Asia Minor. Amber beads discovered at Ulu Burun are thought to be of Baltic origin, while there are large quantities of copper ingots from Cyprus and of tin, perhaps from Afghanistan. Ebony-like wood may have been brought to the coast from central Africa. The ship also carried ivory in the form of elephant tusks, and glass. Part of the vessel itself has been preserved, too, by sea-bed sediment. From these remnants of mortice-and-tenon jointed hull planks, archaeologists can hazard a guess at what the ship may have looked like.

Both its age and its rich cargo give the Ulu Burun ship a special place in marine archaeology – a science that has developed really only since the Second World War. The inventions of self-contained underwater breathing apparatus (SCUBA), radar, sonar, and, later, remote-controlled exploration equipment have opened up the sea-bed and the wrecks upon it in a way that was not possible even a few decades ago. One dramatic example of the advances came in 1985, when a French-American team pinpointed and photographed the wreck of the *Titanic*, which foundered in 13,000 feet of water 560 miles off Newfoundland in 1912. Its many wealthy passengers reputedly had jewelry and other valuables with them when the *Titanic* sank; one voyager is said to have put uncut diamonds worth over $7 million into the security of the *Titanic*'s safe.

Because, as Ulu Burun shows dramatically, there have been valuable shipwrecks for 3,500 years and more, and yet the technology for finding and reaching many of them has evolved only recently, the floors of the world's seas and oceans are probably our greatest remaining repositories of hidden treasures.

TOP-HEAVY TITANS

A gold finger-ring bearing the initials LCD found 90 feet down in the icy waters of the Baltic Sea off Sweden tells a poignant story of the pride of kings. For the ring is one of 17,000 items – including several hundred coins, weaponry, ceremonial armor, and seals – recovered since 1980 from the wreck of the *Kronan*, once the flagship of King Karl XI's Swedish navy.

The massive *Kronan*, 200 feet long and 2,350 tons in weight, was lost in battle with a combined Dutch and Danish fleet on June 1, 1676. On board when she sank were a 550-man crew and 300 marines – and the Swedish admiral Baron Lorentz Creutz. The ring originally belonged to his wife Elsa Duvall, who had died a year earlier. On her death, Creutz had evidently had it enlarged so he could wear it as a

memento. The keepsake went with him to his own watery fate.

The wreck of the *Kronan* was traced, more than 200 years after she capsized, by the naval historian and engineer Anders Franzen. The huge stock of precious and everyday artifacts since salvaged from her outstrip even those from an earlier Franzen find beneath the Baltic, the *Wasa*. That, too, was a Swedish flagship, though of an earlier epoch than the *Kronan*. The *Wasa*, a floating palace with a richly carved stern, went down near Stockholm in 1628 on her maiden voyage. She was raised in 1959, restored, and put on display by Stockholm harbor.

Both the *Kronan* and the *Wasa* stand as monuments to the follies of European monarchs and those who served them. For, in their desire to build ever more-impres-

sive symbols of their sea power, they created huge floating fortresses to support their conventional warships. These monsters, already cumbersome, were made top-heavy by the huge weight of cannon crammed on board – 126 guns weighing 240 tons on the *Kronan*, about one-third of that armory on the much-smaller *Wasa*. If they turned suddenly or heeled in a wind, they sank.

The wreck of the *Wasa* was traced in the 1950s with the help of a core sampler, a device for obtaining specimens of the sea-bed for analysis. The *Mary Rose* was tracked down by divers using modern diving equipment, while underwater, remote-control TV pinpointed the last resting place of the *Kronan*. These technological aids, and others such as powerful suction pumps to clear sand or silt, make wreck location and salvage far easier than it was. But as an occupation, wreck diving is centuries old – as the case of William Phips and the *Nuestra Señora de la Concepción* shows.

THE MARY ROSE

A similar fate befell the *Mary Rose*, pride of the English navy at the time of King Henry VIII. At 600 tons, she was not comparable in size to the 1,400-ton *Wasa*, let alone the *Kronan*. But she had been adapted to carry 60 cannon, some of which were fired through ports in the hull. A breeze heeled her over in Portsmouth harbor in June 1545, with the loss of more than 600 lives. Since her relocation below 15 feet of mud in 1965, the *Mary Rose* has yielded many 16th-century artifacts, including weaponry and rare musical instruments.

LEFT The wooden gun-carriages of the "Wasa" together supported 80 tons of cannon. Their weight made the 120ft (35m) vessel unstable, to the point where a sudden gust of wind capsized her.

A YANKEE PIONEER

The Caribbean Sea and its adjoining waters are as much a hunting ground for sunken treasure ships as they are for hidden pirate gold – and for the same reason. The area was the most hazardous stage on the homeward voyage for Spanish vessels carrying colonial spoils from Latin America between the 16th and the 19th centuries.

The earliest great wreck of a Spanish treasure fleet occurred in July 1502, when 26 ships were sunk by a hurricane in the Mona Passage, between Hispaniola (modern-day Haiti and the Dominican Republic) and Puerto Rico. They were carrying an estimated $2 million in coins and a vast solid gold table said to weigh 3,000 pounds. Christopher Columbus himself, ashore in Hispaniola at the time, had warned the fleet not to sail because of bad weather. Much of the treasure, including the table, and 17 of the ships have never been found.

One early scientific attempt at treasure salvage also took place off Hispaniola, on the Silver Bank, where the *Nuestra Señora de la Concepción* foundered in 1641. Some years later, King Charles II of England financed an expedition, led by the New England merchant William Phips, to recover the cargo of silver.

Phips employed several hundred local divers to descend to the Spanish wreck, protecting them against marauders with two heavily armed vessels. The ingenious Phips also devised a system of diving bells – large barrels lowered into the sea with air trapped inside. Once those were positioned close to the sea-bed, the divers could refill their lungs from the trapped air instead of having to swim right back to the surface.

By such methods, Phips recovered about 35 tons of silver and gold bars, coins, and plate in three months in 1687. That was far from the whole cargo, but the rest lay in the stern of the ship, already heavily encrusted with weed and coral. Nevertheless, King Charles was highly satisfied, rewarding Phips with a knighthood and making him Governor of Massachusetts. Later attempts to raise the remainder of the silver from the *Concepción* included one by the underwater pioneer Jacques Cousteau. He spent several months diving in the area without obtaining treasure, only to discover, from a cannon dated 1756, that his team were working on another, unknown, vessel.

THE OLD SPANIARD'S GOLD

Phips was by no means the first to organize dives to sunken treasure ships. Three wrecks located near Bermuda in the 1950s by the young diver Teddy Tucker had evidently been stripped of many of their valuables soon after they foundered around the beginning of the 17th century. Nevertheless, Tucker discovered jewelry and silver coins overlooked by early salvagers of the *San Antonio* and, on a vessel he nicknamed the *"Old Spaniard,"* a 32-ounce gold bar, pearl-studded gold buttons, and a magnificent gold cross set with emeralds, dating from the 16th century.

TOP RIGHT King Charles II, like other cash-strapped British monarchs before and after him, was not averse to financing treasure hunts. His Hispaniola venture yielded 35 tons of silver and gold in 1687.

TOP LEFT The waters around Hispaniola are littered with the wrecks of treasure-ships. Tortuga Isle, off the northwest coast of what is now Haiti, became a notorious pirate haven soon after it was mapped in 1597.

RIGHT In the warm Caribbean, objects lost under water, such as this pair of cannons, quickly become encrusted with coral and weed. An expert's eye is needed to spot them on the seabed.

GOLDEN DRAGON OF FLORIDA

RIGHT The lighthouse at Key Biscayne is a reminder of how treacherous the Florida coast can prove to vessels under sail. Three entire Spanish treasure-fleets lost off Florida in the 17th and 18th centuries have been relocated since 1949.

'What kind of dinner can a man eat to pick his teeth with that?" exulted Florida builder Kip Wagner over a 250-year-old, solid-gold toothpick rescued from the ocean depths and valued at a minimum of $50,000. The pick, fitted inside a gold, dragon-shaped whistle held on a 2,176-link gold chain and probably once the property of a Spanish fleet commander, is one of the most unusual items found in one of the most extraordinary underwater recovery operations yet mounted. The target of the search was virtually an entire Spanish plate fleet (11 ships) that came to grief in a hurricane off Florida in 1715.

Historical records show that the Spanish authorities moved quickly to retrieve the sunken treasure, spread over the sandy sea-bed from Cape Canaveral to Fort Pierce Inlet. They hired some 300 Indians to dive to the wrecks, kept them at work for four years, and pronounced themselves satisfied that most of the precious cargo had been rescued. Then the fleet was largely forgotten for more than two centuries, to the point that no one was sure where precisely it had gone down.

Kip Wagner became obsessed with the fleet's fate when he discovered seven silver coins on the beach at Sebastian in 1948. Secretly, he studied archive records of the disaster, and wind and wave action on Florida's Atlantic coast. But his biggest clue to the whereabouts of the wrecks came when he located the remains of the base used by the Spanish and their local divers during the 18th-century salvage mission, near Sebastian. With this reference point, and the help of amateur divers, Wagner was able to locate most of the sunken vessels. Since 1959, they have yielded a priceless haul to which treasure is still being added. For the original salvors had been unable to find part of the ships' cargoes in the murky waters, some of which they had not looked for: they had not taken into account the seamen's risky habit of smuggling aboard precious items on their own account, that carried the death penalty in 18th-century Spain.

Other items included gold bars, gold necklaces, and diamond rings, as well as the admiral's chain, dragon whistle, and toothpick. Amazingly, 28 vases of delicate Chinese porcelain had also survived the wreck and 250 years' immersion in the hurricane-tossed Florida waters.

FAR RIGHT Until 1728, the Spanish minted their silver pieces-of-eight in crude shapes. This one, shown front and back, was recovered from a treasure-wreck and is dated 1714.

BELOW A 17th-century Spanish plate fleet assembles at Havana, Cuba, before sailing in convoy across the Atlantic. The galleons, heavy with gold and silver, were escorted by fighting ships.

A THOUSAND GOLD COINS

In one day's diving alone, Wagner's team retrieved more than 1,000 gold coins. Thousands of silver pieces-of-eight were found scattered in the sea-bed sand, or fused together in the shape of the canvas bags or wooden chests in which they had been stored. One wooden treasure chest – about 3 feet long – was even discovered intact, with 3,000 silver coins still inside.

FIND THE *ATOCHA*!

The laden Spanish plate fleets that enticed Kip Wagner to perform his feats of discovery have been a powerful lure for many others, too. None has pursued the quest more single-mindedly than the American engineer and diving expert Mel Fisher. In 1973, Fisher began to reap the reward of more than a decade's endeavors, when his team located the wreck of the *Nuestra Señora de Atocha* near the Marquesas Keys off the tip of Florida. The Spanish vessel was one of 15 to founder there in 1622, among them also the *Margarita*, which Fisher traced later.

However, it was not until 1985 that full details of the *Atocha*'s magnificent cargo really became clear. The coins, bullion, and other precious items aboard were estimated to be worth $450 million – the most valuable load yet found on a single plate ship.

Fisher nearly bankrupted himself on various occasions in the hunt for the *Atocha*, partly because, for several years he had been diving in the wrong spot. Painstaking research in old Spanish records finally showed the ship went down about 100 miles to the west of the original search area. There was personal tragedy, too; Fisher's son Dirk and his daughter-in-law were aboard a search vessel that sank in a storm. Then Fisher was drawn into a court battle with the state of Florida

RIGHT Slight dents around the rim are the only indication that this golden plate from the Atocha *lay beneath the Atlantic waves for 350 years.*

RIGHT Wreck-hunter extraordinaire Mel Fisher in 1985 with a magnificent gold chain and other items from the Atocha. The stupendous cargo, valued at $450 million, is the richest yet recovered from a single Spanish treasure-ship.

in 1949 by a local diver, Arthur McKee, and several other vessels of the same period have been located since, for example at Tavernier. However, they went down in relatively shallow, clear water, so divers probably salvaged most of their cargoes almost immediately. The presumed wreck of the *Rui* nevertheless yielded some gold and silver coins, jewelry, cannons, muskets, pistols – and a silver statuette of a Spanish flamenco dancer.

over the ownership of the treasure. It took him five years to prove title to his finds, but he finally became free to sell some of them and make plans to display the rest publicly in a museum at Key West.

The wrecks of 1715, located by Kip Wagner, and of 1622, found by Mel Fisher, were two of the biggest natural disasters to strike the Spanish plate fleets. Another occurred in 1733, when some 20 ships were lost in a hurricane, also off the Florida Keys. What are thought to be the remains of the 1733 fleet's flagship, the *Rui*, were discovered

ABOVE A sumptuous gold cross, set with pearls, may once have belonged to a prince of the Spanish church. Treasures from the Atocha are now on display at Key West, Florida.

LEFT Chests bulging with silver coins are everyone's dream of Spanish treasure. Mel Fisher's single-minded quest for the wreck of the Atocha turned his dream into reality in 1973.

TRACING THE ARMADA

RIGHT The Spanish Armada was, in its day, the mightiest battle fleet ever seen.

When the Spanish set out to subdue England in 1588, the 125-ship Armada they assembled for the task was not only a mighty battle fleet, but also a symbol of Spain's vast wealth at that time in her history. Aboard one galleon – variously known as the *Florida*, the *San Francisco,* or the *Duque de Florencia* – was a fortune in gold and silver coins, worth perhaps $150 million at today's values and intended to pay the fleet's 30,000 men. Aboard others, rich and aristocratic Spanish naval commanders had their personal jewelry and precious items near them in their cabins.

In a running battle that lasted the best part of two weeks, the Armada was defeated by the English navy, losing perhaps 25 ships. One was the *Nuestra Señora del Rosario*; the veteran English privateer Sir Francis Drake took time off from the fighting to escort her to harbor – and to help himself to the treasure she carried.

Once the outcome of the battle became clear, the Spanish commander, the Duke of Medina Sidonia, made a fateful decision. Instead of scurrying back to Spain by the shortest route, he ordered the surviving ships to sail around the British Isles, on a course that took them through some of the world's most treacherous waters. As a result, another 20-25 vessels were wrecked. The hunt for their treasures began almost immediately, and continues today.

The *Florida*, with its vast pay chest, went down in Tobermory Bay, Scotland. Attempts to salvage her gold and silver have been taking place off and on at least since 1640. But so far the most spectacular item recovered is a bronze cannon said to have been cast by the Italian sculptor Benvenuto Cellini.

The wreck of the three-masted *Girona* has yielded much more impressive finds. The Belgian diver Robert Sténuit found her in 1967 off Lacada Point, County Antrim, Northern Ireland, and was astonished by the riches she carried – some of them rescued from other Armada ships which went down before she did. The *Girona* treasure includes 1,200 gold and silver coins, but pride of place goes to the jewelry and other decorative items. There is a cameo brooch mounted and set in pure gold decorated with eight pearls, and another brooch depicting a salamander, also of gold and originally set with eight rubies, of which three were still in place when Sténuit retrieved it.

The success of the *Girona* expedition put new life into the Armada treasure hunt. Known wreck sites include Fair Isle in the Shetlands, Kinnagoe Bay and Strcedagh Bay in Ireland, and Hope Cove in Devon, England. But there could be anything up to three dozen others around the coasts of the British Isles. Not all are likely to be as rich as the *Girona* has proved to be and the *Florida* reputedly was; nearly half of

the Armada vessels were supply and support ships, rather than galleons and armed merchantmen. When the *Santa Maria de la Rosa* was found in 1968 near Great Blasket Isle in Ireland, the only "treasure" was a few coins, a medallion, and some pewter plates.

THE TREACHEROUS ISLANDS

A rough granite monument at Porth Hellick recalls one of the most notorious shipwrecks – and treasure hunts – in the Scillies, a tiny but treacherous group of islands off the southwest tip of Britain where more than 800 vessels are known to have sunk over the centuries. The memorial marks what is said to have been the temporary grave of Sir Cloudesley Shovell, commander-in-chief of the British Mediterranean fleet in 1707.

Shovell was returning to England with 21 ships after naval campaigns against the French and Spanish when, through navigational error, five vessels foundered on

LEFT Gold and silver coins from the $3 million cargo of the Association, *wrecked off the Isles of Scilly as a result of navigational error in 1707.*

reefs near the Scillies and went to the bottom. One was Shovell's flagship, the *Association*, laden with over $3 million in bullion and silver. About 2,000 seamen drowned. Shovell himself is reputed to

THE FLAGSHIP'S RICHES

The exact site of the wreck of the *Association*, and its treasure, remained obscure for more than two centuries. Some believe that the local people deliberately concealed its whereabouts so they could plunder it undisturbed. But in 1967 a Royal Navy diving team found it, with vast numbers of 17th-century gold and silver coins, bronze cannon, ship's objects, and, eventually, a silver plate bearing Shovell's personal crest. Naïvely, the find was widely publicized from the beginning, so dozens of authorized and unauthorized divers descended on the site, ransacking it without always declaring their prizes. As a result, no one can be absolutely sure how much treasure was recovered. But informed estimates put it at about one-third of the original cargo; the rest may have been quietly removed much earlier, or may remain under the turbulent Atlantic waters.

have reached the shore only to be murdered, as he lay exhausted above the waterline, by a local woman who stole his jeweled rings. His body was concealed in the sand, and exhumed when the murderess confessed many years later.

Since the discovery of the *Association*, several other treasure ships have been located and salvaged in the Scillies. One of the most spectacular is the *Hollandia*, a Dutch East Indiaman which sank in 1743 and was traced in 1971. Divers extracted from her thousands and thousands of silver coins, mostly pieces-of-eight minted by the Spanish in Mexico City and European-minted ducatoons or "silvery riders"; all were intended by the Dutch East India Company to finance its trade in the Far East. In 1969, the *Romney*, a sister ship of Shovell's *Association*, yielded gold coins, silver pieces-of-eight, and jewelry, including a wedding band with the inscription "in thy sight is my delight."

Treasures of a different sort – priceless Classical vases – were recovered from 1975 from the remains of the *Colossus,* which had foundered in the Scillies in 1798. Wrecks that remain to be traced in the area include the *Eagle,* another of Sir

ABOVE A diver raises artifacts from the Liefde, *which capsized in the Shetland Isles in 1711. Records suggest her cargo included 227,000 silver coins, but relatively few have been found.*

RIGHT Pipe bowls, spoons, plates, and other objects from the wreck of the Liefde. *The 500-ton Dutch East Indiaman had a crew of 200 under Captain Barent Muijkens, and there were 100 soldiers aboard.*

Cloudesley Shovell's ships, and the *Merchant Royal*, lost in 1641 with silver, gold, and jewels worth perhaps as much as $5 million today.

At the opposite end of Britain from the Isles of Scilly, the Shetland Isles had an equally fearsome reputation among seafarers in the days of sail. Two Dutch East Indiamen lost there – the *Kennermerlandt,* which sank in 1664, and the *Liefde*, which went down close to the earlier wreck in 1711 – have been the targets of almost continuous salvage attempts ever since. Like the *Hollandia* in the Scillies, they were carrying huge amounts of silver coins, but surprisingly few are recorded as found. A treasure chest and some loose coins were recovered in the 1960s and other items, such as the ship's bell from the *Liefde,* have also been raised.

EASTERN PROMISE

LEFT Porcelain and rare ingots of Chinese gold survived ocean immersion for more than 200 years, to be recovered in 1985 from the wreck of the East Indiaman Geldermalsen.

Blue-and-white Chinese porcelain may not match the traditional idea of hidden treasure, but when it is two centuries old, perfectly preserved despite immersion in salt water for most of its life, and there are 100,000 pieces, it is worth millions – more than $15 million, to be precise. That was the sum achieved at auction in Amsterdam in 1986 for what became known as the "Nanking cargo," the contents of the Dutch East Indiaman *Geldermalsen*, wrecked in 1752 at the entrance to the Malacca Strait between Malaya and Sumatra.

Like the Caribbean in the western Atlantic, the seas around what is now Indonesia, where the Pacific and Indian Oceans meet, were a vital trade crossroads from the 16th to the 19th centuries. Ships of Portugal, Holland, and Britain plowed the waters, laden mostly with silver on the outward voyage, and with gold, spices, ivory, gems, and other commodities on the return.

Many came to grief because of storms, treacherous currents, and reefs – the *Geldermalsen* among them.

The wreck of the *Geldermalsen* was rediscovered in 1985 by the British salvage expert Michael Hatcher. At the time, he was one of few people to appreciate the potential value of cargoes of antique porcelain. Some two years earlier, he had recovered 23,000 items of Ming china from a 17th-century Asian trading junk in the vicinity, and those sold for $3 million. The *Geldermalsen* put Hatcher's previous find well and truly in the shade.

The vast assembly of porcelain items – 40,000 tea dishes with saucers and enough lavish dinner settings for a public banquet – had been packed in chests of tea (another valuable commodity) for the voyage back to Europe. With this protection, the china remained in mint condition on the sea-bed for 233 years. That was not all Hatcher found; scattered around the wreck were more than 100 small ingots of Chinese gold, cast in the 18th century and of types not previously known in the West.

Hatcher's success, like similar operations elsewhere, stimulated a host of copycat endeavors in the same area, not all of them officially licensed or scientifically

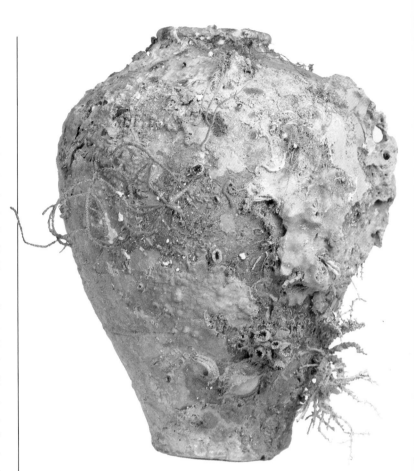

conducted. In some cases, rival teams of unscrupulous treasure raiders were said to have threatened each other with death in their greed for the biggest prize of all – the wreck of the Portuguese carrack *Flor del Mar*.

That went down somewhere off the northwest coast of Sumatra in January 1512, carrying vast quantities of booty taken by the Portuguese admiral Alfonso de Albuquerque from the sultanate of Malacca in what is now Malaysia, after a 12-day siege and large-scale slaughter. The spoils reputedly include 20 or more tons of gold in the form of animal statues, chests brimming with gems, tons of Arab and Chinese coins, jewelry, plate, and other valuables. Conservative archaeologists have given estimates of the present-day value at between $2 billion and $9 billion. Others claim it could be worth up to as much as $80 billion, but even the lowest figure would be an all-time record haul from a single wreck. By the end of 1989, the *Flor del Mar* had still not been found.

RIGHT The sheer scale of the Nanking Cargo makes it one of the most impressive of all underwater finds. The pattern on the tea bowls and saucers is known as "Pagoda Riverscape."

MODERN TIMES

The storm-lashed, icy waters of the Barents Sea, inside the Arctic Circle north of Norway, are among the most inhospitable in the world. Few salvagers would choose to work in them – but when the lost treasure at stake is 465 gold ingots worth almost $70 million, some will face any hardship. Keith Jessop, a diver from Yorkshire, England, was one.

For years, Jessop was obsessed by one of the most valuable, and inaccessible, wrecks of modern times, the British Royal Navy cruiser *Edinburgh*. In 1942, at the

ABOVE Loss of the Edinburgh *was reported in* The Illustrated London News *of May 16, 1942, with this picture, but no mention was made of her $70 million cargo of gold.*

height of the Second World War, the *Edinburgh* was transporting gold ingots in secrecy from Murmansk in Russia, as part-payment to the United States for armaments supplied to the Soviet Union in the struggle against Hitler's Germany. The bullion-laden cruiser was ostensibly one of the escorts for an Allied convoy returning from Murmansk. In the Barents Sea, the ships came under prolonged German naval attack, and the badly damaged *Edinburgh* eventually had to be scuppered

with her gold, to prevent her falling into enemy hands. At that point, 57 of her 700 crew were dead. The survivors were taken off by other Allied craft before the *Edinburgh* received the *coup de grâce* from the British destroyer *Foresight*.

To set about recovering the gold, nearly 40 years afterward, Jessop had first to overcome the reluctance of the British authorities, who had declared the *Edinburgh* a war grave, and the suspicions of the Soviets, who retained a partial claim on the bullion. He also had to locate the wreck precisely, and to be ready to dive on it when the weather was least hostile, in September. Eventually he overcame all these obstacles, using underwater video and sonar to pinpoint the remains of the Edinburgh 800 feet down. In partnership with the British company Wharton-Williams, who supplied the recovery vessel *Stephaniturm*, Jessop began the rescue in September 1981. The team of divers operated from a diving bell; in three weeks they found and raised 431 of the 465 ingots – an incredible feat in the conditions.

Jessop got only $2.5 million for his perseverance. About $20 million went to the Soviet Union, $11 million to Britain, and some $22 million to Wharton-Williams for their technical support. But the Yorkshireman also had the satisfaction of initiating an underwater recovery at a depth never previously matched and only now being exceeded.

Another wartime victim to inspire fervor equaling Jessop's is the passenger liner *Lusitania*, sunk without warning by a German torpedo in 1915 in St. George's Channel, between Britain and Ireland. Out of about 2,000 people aboard, more than

LEFT The sinking of the passenger liner Lusitania *in 1915 cost 1,198 lives. The hunt for the bullion she is said to have carried continues 75 years later.*

half perished, of whom more than 100 were American; the attack helped to persuade the U.S. to enter the First World War. The *Lusitania* is known to have been carrying a valuable collection of paintings, and rumored also to have been shipping millions of dollars' worth of gold bullion across the Atlantic. Despite intensive searches that have gone on since the 1960s, no trace of the bullion has yet been found. However, parts of the ship itself and everyday shipboard items have acquired considerable value because of the *Lusitania*'s fame – raising $5 million or so to defray the gold-searchers' costs.

The "Lusitania" (German) Medal

An exact replica of the medal which was designed in Germany and distributed to commemorate the sinking of the "Lusitania."

This indicates the true feeling the War Lords endeavour to stimulate, and is proof positive that such crimes are not merely regarded favourably, but are given every encouragement in the land of Kultur.

The "Lusitania" was sunk by a German submarine on May 7th, 1915. She had on board at the time 1,951 passengers and crew, of whom 1,198 perished.

LEFT The Germans struck a medal after the Lusitania *was torpedoed by one of their submarines during the First World War. British and U.S. opinion was outraged by the attack.*

LEFT Fewer than 800 of the Lusitania's *passengers and crew survived. Many of the ship's lifeboats were washed ashore empty on the Irish coast.*

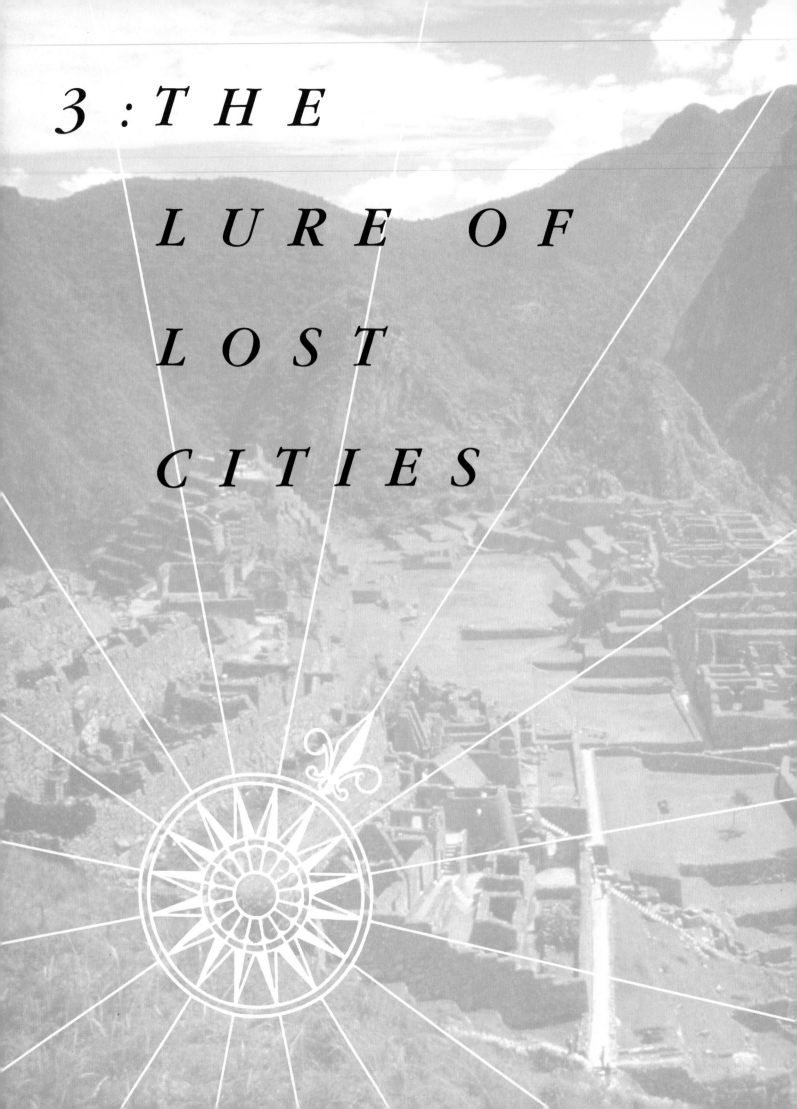

3 : THE LURE OF LOST CITIES

Tales of long-lost, treasure-laden cities and kingdoms abound on every continent. But only the most die-hard of sceptics dares dismiss them out of hand since Heinrich Schliemann confounded the scoffers a century ago by rediscovering the site of ancient Troy. Time and nature between them can obliterate all but the smallest traces of man's most durable structures. Often, though, their former presence lingers on in folk-memory.

Sometimes the memory becomes distorted by layers of myth. So it was with one of the most durable tales of all – the lost, gold-rich "land" of El Dorado. Experts have now peeled off the layers, which once led hundreds of fortune hunters to their deaths.

Sometimes the memory is surprisingly accurate, as it was in Schliemann's case and that of Stephens and Lloyd, whose explorations began the recovery of knowledge about the mysterious Maya civilization. A perennial quest is for Ophir, the source of King Solomon's vast wealth as recounted in the Bible. Cecil Rhodes believed he had discovered it in central Africa at the end of the last century. In December 1989, newspaper reports suggested it might have been traced in the jungles of Peru, where the American explorer Gene Savoy is credited with finding no fewer than 40 lost cities already . . . .

IN THE STEPS OF ODYSSEUS

For centuries, men and women have been enthralled by Homer's epic poems the *Iliad* and the *Odyssey,* written more than 2,500 years ago. The abduction of the beautiful Helen from the Greek city of Sparta by Paris of Troy, the war between Greece and Troy that followed, and the subsequent wanderings of some of the victorious Greeks under their leader Odysseus are the very essence of heroic myth – or so people generally believed.

Then, in the 1870s, a swaggering self-made millionaire, Heinrich Schliemann, confounded received wisdom. He helped to prove Homer's works are based on fact, by tracing the long-lost city of Troy itself. As a bonus, he turned up magnificent treasure that remains a source of mystery today.

Schliemann was born in 1822 in Neubuckow, Germany. From childhood, when he was given an illustrated edition of Homer's works, he was passionately interested in the Trojan War. Unlike most of his contemporaries, he was convinced that the poems – which are quite detailed in some of their geographical descriptions – told of real places and real events, even though highly exaggerated. By 1870, Schliemann had made his fortune trading in America and Russia, and he was free to pursue this conviction full time.

In the *Iliad,* Homer is precise about the location of Troy, by the flood plain of the River Scamander (now the Menderes), opposite the Hellespont (the Dardanelles), in northwestern Turkey. Schliemann headed there, to the village of Hissarlik, where a nearby mound seemed a likely

LEFT Heinrich Schliemann (1822–90) overturned the popular beliefs of his day by discovering the location of Homer's Troy. More than 8,000 ancient gold items appeared during the excavations.

place to start digging for traces of Troy. The discovery of masonry and rubble just below the surface suggested he was on the right track.

The enthusiastic German was no painstaking modern archaeologist. With the help of local workmen, he crashed further and further into the mound, through layers of masonry 50 feet deep. What he was looking for was evidence of the fire which, again according to Homer, swept Troy after the Greeks had tricked their way into the city using their giant wooden horse. He found it, and quickly announced his success through a stream of bulletins to newspapers.

Then, in 1873, came a greater triumph – the discovery of gold artifacts which, Schliemann decided, were the treasure of King Priam, ruler of Troy at the time of the Greek siege. Day after day, more of these priceless objects were uncovered; day after day, Schliemann announced the latest finds to an increasingly fascinated

LEFT Schliemann's frenetic digging revealed no fewer than nine ancient cities built successively on the same Turkish site. He misjudged which one was Homeric Troy.

BELOW The legendary wooden horse the Greeks used to trick their way into Troy is depicted on a pithos – a ceramic vessel to hold oil or grain. It dates from the 7th century BC.

world. The eventual tally was stupendous – more than 8,000 gold items, including necklaces and bracelets, cups and vases. Schliemann draped some of the jewelry on his wife Sophia, for photographs. Finally, he arranged for the whole hoard to be secretly shipped from Turkey to Germany, where it ended up in the Ethnological Museum in Berlin.

Later research has indicated that Schliemann's Trojan gold was up to 1,000 years older than he thought. Quite possibly, it was lost centuries before Priam ruled the city. There are even suggestions that part

of it was brought to Hissarlik from elsewhere while Schliemann's dig went on, to boost his self-admitted desire for publicity. Schliemann was wrong, too, about Homeric Troy. Though he had found its location, he had dug through its remains to reach a previous settlement on the site, which altogether had been inhabited for 4,000 years. Despite these doubts, and his heavy-handed methods which destroyed much of archaeological value, Schliemann had fulfilled his life's quest. Even so, there was more in store for him – and for his treasure.

LEFT Sophia Schliemann modeled priceless ancient jewelry, found by her husband, for photographs and engravings. The luxurious head-dress and necklaces, from Mycenae, have been dated to about 1550 BC.

HOME OF HEROES

RIGHT The remains of the acropolis, or citadel, at Mycenae. Here Schliemann found another spectacular collection of ancient gold, and clues to a long-forgotten civilization.

BELOW Schliemann believed this priceless golden death mask was that of King Agamemnon. In fact, it is perhaps 300 years older than Schliemann thought, but it certainly shows a rich and powerful ruler.

The city of Mycenae plays its part in Homeric and other tales of ancient Greece as the capital of King Agamemnon, leader of the Greek army at the siege of Troy, murdered by his wife on his victorious homecoming. Fired with success from the rediscovery of Troy, Heinrich Schliemann set out in the 1870s to trace Agamemnon's last resting place. In the process, the German amateur archaeologist unearthed his second find of magnificent treasure, and a key to an entire civilization.

The location of Mycenae, unlike that of Troy, was known in Schliemann's day. Its ruined acropolis, or citadel, still commands the plain of Argos on the Peloponnesian pensinsula of mainland Greece. Schliemann began to dig in the citadel, near the huge Lion Gate. Soon he discovered a circle of upright stones, then gravestones, and finally graves cut deep into the underlying rock.

His wife Sophia was the first to spot gold, shining in the earth. It was a ring. As

DEATH MASK OF A KING

One of the masks stood out from the rest by its sharp features and cruel mouth. Raising it, Schliemann found the flesh intact – or so he said. "I have gazed on the face of Agamemnon," read the telegram he then fired off to the King of Greece.

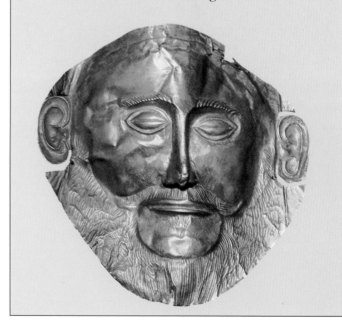

work progressed, Schliemann uncovered 19 skeletons, several of them wearing stupendous gold armor, gold death masks, and jewelry.

As with Troy, Schliemann's romantic assumptions have subsequently been shown to be wrong in detail, if not in general thrust. The exquisite gold objects of Mycenae and other remains are several centuries older than he thought, and pre-date the siege of Troy. A ransacked tomb

ABOVE A bronze cuirass (body armor) and helmet made from boars' tusks, from the Mycenaean period of ancient Greece. Chieftains were buried in gold armor.

culture based on Crete, which reached its peak about 1950 BC.

The spectacular Schliemann finds from Mycenae are now on show in Greece's National Archaeological Museum in Athens, where the death masks and other gold items alone occupy several display cases. But the whereabouts of his 8,000-piece golden hoard from the site of Troy are a mystery. The entire glittering collection was taken from the Berlin museum and hidden for safekeeping during the Second World War, and has not been heard of since the Soviets entered Berlin in 1945. Perhaps, in the age of *glasnost*, a latter-day Schliemann can again track the Trojan treasure down.

ABOVE The royal grave circle dug by Schliemann at Mycenae is one of two in the ruins. It contained 19 skeletons, two of children, in six graves – and a dazzling array of golden grave goods.

BELOW A Mycenaean vase on display in the National Museum, Athens, shows spear-carrying warriors of ancient Greece. It dates from the 13th or 12th century BC.

below the citadel is now announced to visitors as that of Agamemnon.

Nevertheless, Schliemann's pioneering enthusiasm proved the existence of highly developed Bronze Age civilizations in the region of the Aegean long before the age of Classical Greece. His activities led directly to present-day knowledge of the Mycenaean culture (named from Mycenae), which flourished for about 500 years from 1600 BC. Indirectly, they contributed to the discovery of the Minoan

THE QUEST FOR EL DORADO

'Gold is the most exquisite of all things," declared Christopher Columbus some 500 years ago, when his voyages were opening up the New World for Spain. "Whoever possesses gold can acquire all that he desires in the world. Truly, for gold he can gain entrance for his soul into Paradise."

With hindsight, Columbus's words drip under the weight of doom. The conquistadors who followed in his wake to the Americas seemed to take them literally. In their insatiable hunger for gold and other precious commodities, they pillaged entire ancient civilizations and slaughtered mercilessly foes – or friends – who stood in their way. Some amassed vast personal fortunes and survived to spend them; a few of those, perhaps seeking atonement and to buy entry to some Columbian Paradise, endowed rich churches. Many others died deaths as hard as they had meted out in their greed. Always, though, gold fever drove them on.

Among the first of the Spanish invaders was Hernán Cortés, conqueror of Montezuma's Aztecs in what is now Mexico.

BELOW Cortés, conqueror of Mexico, meets Guantemoc, a local ruler, at the beginning of the Spanish invasion of the Americas. Driven by gold-fever, the Spaniards ransacked a continent . . . and were still unsatisfied.

RIGHT Hernán Cortés (1485–1547) landed in Mexico in 1519 with just 508 followers. Within two years, they had overthrown the gold-rich Aztec empire, whose warriors had no answer to the Spaniards' firearms and horses.

Close behind him was Francisco Pizarro, who overthrew Atahualpa's Inca in what is now Peru. Between them, this pair largely subdued two of the wealthiest and most powerful empires on an entire continent in little more than a dozen years from 1519.

Plundered riches began to flow almost from the start of the conquests, in quantities to impress the most rapacious. The notorious Pizarro used a combination of blackmail and double-cross to extract 11 tons of gold and 12 tons of silver from the Inca during six months of 1533. Later, when sacking the Inca capital of Cuzco, he took nearly 3 tons of gold and 50 tons of silver in a matter of days, as a prelude

RIGHT Francisco Pizarro (1470?–1541) had only about 180 men under his command when he launched the conquest of Peru in 1530. Rapacious and brutal, he was eventually assassinated by his own followers.

FAR RIGHT Some of the pre-Columbian civilizations of the Americas showed considerable skill and artistry in working gold and silver. The invading Spaniards melted down many objects of beauty. A few, such as these golden grave goods from Colombia, survive intact.

to two years' systematic pillage of the Inca territories. Often, the gold and silver was in the form of priceless artifacts, which the conquistadors melted down by the thousand to make them easier to transport.

Wealth-stripping on such a huge scale needed to be put on an organized footing. By the mid-16th century, the Spanish had set up land and sea routes, bringing the loot to assembly points at their new Caribbean ports of Cartagena in Colombia and Portobelo in Panama. From there, it was shipped back to Spain in heavily protected plate fleets. The outward flow of treasure was to continue for more than 200 years.

But none of this was enough for the gold-hungry conquistadors. They reasoned that if the territories they first conquered could yield such spoils, much more must lie elsewhere. Expeditions began moving further and further through the Americas in the gold quest.

Soon, the expeditionaries encountered strange rumors of a local king whose coronation rites required him to be coated from head to toe in gold dust, which he washed off in the waters of a lake while his subjects threw piles of gold and emeralds into it as offerings to the gods. Thus began the legend of "the man of gold" – *El Dorado*. It did not stop there. The tales got ever more extravagant in the telling, the king's capital became a city with streets and houses of solid gold, and gradually the El Dorado of the original reports was transformed from a man into a place. As such, it became an objective for the roamings of the conquistadors over much of South and Central America, and even in what is now the southwestern United States. Hundreds, possibly thousands, of people lost their lives in the search for El Dorado.

Not all were Spanish, as other European powers quickly came to envy Spain its American sources of wealth. Perhaps the most famous name in the whole, centuries-long El Dorado quest is that of an Englishman – the founder of Virginia, Sir Walter Raleigh.

SIR WALTER'S TRAGIC DREAM

O f the rival powers to cast envious eyes on Spain's American loot, none was more covetous than England. Throughout most of the 16th century, partly for religious reasons, the Roman Catholic Spanish were, to the English, the enemy. Even when the two countries were technically at peace, Spanish settlements and ships were considered fair game by buccaneering English sea dogs such as Sir Francis Drake.

Drake's many feats against the Spanish included the capture of the treasure ship *Cacafuego* in the Pacific in 1579 and the holding for ransom of the entire treasure port of Cartagena in 1586. But Drake contented himself with gadfly attacks. His younger contemporary, Sir Walter Raleigh, was far more ambitious – and his ambition cost him his head.

Rich and accomplished, but arrogant, Raleigh seesawed in both royal and popular esteem from the time he rose to prominence as a favorite of the Virgin

Queen, Elizabeth I, in 1581. One of his ambitions from the start of his court career seems to have been to establish an English presence in the New World to rival that of Spain. However, his earliest venture in this direction, the creation of the North American colony he named Virginia in honor of Queen Elizabeth, was not an initial success, though he poured a personal fortune into it.

In the early 1590s, Raleigh was involved in fighting the Spanish in the West Indies. Through the capture of a Spanish provincial governor, Antonio de Berrio, he acquired a map purporting to show the location of the fabled golden territory of El Dorado. By then, the legend of an entire city or land of gold, richer than either Peru or Mexico, had taken firm root among the conquistadors. Berrio believed in it, indeed had led three expeditions to look for it. Raleigh believed, too. What better way to redeem the Virginia failure than by finding El Dorado and claiming it for England?

Raleigh organized an expedition in 1594-96 to the region indicated on the captured map, along the Orinoco River in what is now Venezuela. But the expeditionaries were eventually forced to turn back by lack of supplies, having found nothing but jungle.

Raleigh's prestige at the English court, always erratic, plunged on Elizabeth's death. Her successor, James I, regarded him as a threat. In 1603, Raleigh was found guilty on a fraudulent charge of treason. His death sentence was commuted at the last moment to life imprisonment in the Tower of London. He remained there for 13 years, nurturing his dream until he

BELOW On the first of his two luckless quests for El Dorado, Sir Walter Raleigh (1552?–1618) and his men took the Spanish settlement of St. Joseph, on the island of Trinidad.

LEFT At Trinidad, Raleigh pores over the captured map purporting to show El Dorado. His searches led him, not to a golden land, but to the executioner's block.

persuaded the impoverished King James to let him search for the gold again.

James imposed tough conditions. England was not only at peace with Spain by 1616, but the two countries were allies. Raleigh was ordered, on pain of death, not to clash with the Spanish, in whose territory the Orinoco lay. Raleigh agreed. However, an advance party led by Raleigh's son Wat ignored the deal and attacked the Spanish settlement of San Tomé in Ven-

ezuela. Wat was killed in the fighting. Heartbroken, Raleigh returned to England, to be executed in 1618 because of his son's hotheadedness.

Many other abortive searches for El Dorado followed over the next 200 years. By the 19th century, just as Spain was losing her grip in the Americas, explorers started peeling back the layers of legend. Ironically, the truth had been there to see from the outset.

THE LAKE OF RITUAL

igh in the northeastern fringes of the Andes, near Bogotá in present-day Colombia, lies a chain of steep-sided lakes once sacred to the Muisca (Chibcha) peoples who inhabited the region when the Spanish arrived in the Americas. Like the Inca further south, the Muisca were rich in gold. They worked it into intricate and beautiful objects, certain of which apparently had a ritual purpose. Unlike the Inca, however, the Muisca civilization was already in decline when it became known to Europeans.

Of the lakes, the most sacred was Guatavita. According to reports reaching the Spanish conquistadors by the 1530s, it was the site of the ceremonies attending the coronation of El Dorado, the "man of gold." Some even said rites in which gold and jewels were cast into the waters took place there before dawn on every single day. Whatever the truth, Lake Guatavita was a tempting target for the invaders.

By about 1540, three separate Spanish expeditions had reached the lake. They plundered gold from nearby settlements, but found little or nothing to suggest that Guatavita was the repository of vast riches. Nevertheless, the lake continued to exercise its fascination. In 1544, the Spaniard Hernando Quesada pressed thousands of Muisca into baling out its waters, lowering them by a few feet. From the exposed mud, he recovered small, crude figures of men, some of them in gold. It was hardly a fortune.

A more ambitious effort at draining Guatavita was made in the 1570s by one Antonio de Sepúlveda. He ordered the Muisca to cut a trench in the lake's steep sides through which its waters could escape, and succeeded in lowering the level by perhaps 50 feet. This exposed more crude figures used in rituals, jewelry, and a few gold items. But the trench collapsed as Sepúlveda ordered it to be dug deeper, and with it the whole venture.

At that point, the Spanish largely lost interest in Guatavita. The tale of El Dorado had assumed a life of its own and become a land or city of gold, which the lake was clearly not. The gold hunters turned their attentions elsewhere.

But the lake and its associations were not entirely forgotten. More than two centuries after Sepúlveda, the German scientist and explorer Baron Alexander Von Humboldt helped revive speculation about its mysteries by calculating it could

THE SECRETS OF LAKE GUATAVITA

In the early 1900s, a British company succeeded in draining much of the lake and retrieving more gold items, which were eventually auctioned. However, with the water removed, the deep mud of the lake bed baked rock-hard immediately in the heat, or in some places turned into an impenetrable sludge, thwarting all further exploration. In 1932, an American diver is said to have retrieved death-masks and jewelry from the waters. For the past 25 years, the Colombian government has banned investigations of Lake Guatavita, though a properly mounted archaeological study might gain its approval – and complete our knowledge of El Dorado.

LEFT The scientific explorations of Alexander Von Humboldt (1769–1859) in Central and South America revived interest in the legend of El Dorado. Humboldt visited the Orinoco region, where some believed El Dorado to be, and Lake Guatavita,where the tales probably originated.

hold up to $300 million in gold. In 1856, a gold Muisca relic was found at Lake Siecha nearby; it depicts a king and his attendants on a raft of rushes, an essential element in the El Dorado coronation ritual as described in the earliest accounts. This stylized artifact does more than anything else to suggest the tales of El Dorado which first met the Spanish had a basis in truth. Possibly the rites referred to had already been abandoned before the Spanish invasion, living on only in folk-memory. In any case, the gold raft inspired further expeditions to Lake Guatavita.

SECRET STRONGHOLDS OF THE ANDES

he Inca empire was the largest ever to exist in the Americas, well organized and with a substantial army. Yet for four years it offered little real resistance to Francisco Pizarro's conquistadors while they slaughtered people and plundered precious objects at will.

In 1536, the trance lifted. Manco, an Inca put in as puppet ruler by Pizarro, led an uprising that failed only at the last minute. In any case, the attempt was too late to drive the Spanish away altogether. But for the next 35 years Manco and his successors skirmished from a series of increasingly remote mountain strongholds. The last of those, Vilcabamba, fell only in 1572. The Inca themselves set fire to it when its capture could no longer be prevented.

The Spanish who reached Vilcabamba evidently thought little enough of the place. Its location, like that of some other Inca rebel retreats, was soon forgotten. However, perhaps borrowing from the tales of El Dorado, a legend grew of a "lost city of the Inca" where the last rebels concealed their remaining gold. By the early 19th century, expeditions of treasure hunters were traipsing the Andes looking for it.

Many of these explorers were motivated, like the *conquistadors* before them, purely by gold fever, though a moment's thought would have told them that the last Inca probably had little of value left. Archaeologically important sites such as Sacsahuamanan, Manco's first stronghold near Cuzco, and Choquequirau, suffered from their depredations.

RIGHT The massive stone blocks of the Temple of the Three Windows at Machu Picchu are typical of the Inca building style. Even earthquakes have failed to shift them.

Gradually, however, more responsible investigators took over the search for ancient cities. In the 1870s, the German Max Uhle, the father of Peruvian archaeology, worked on the religious center of Pachacamac, near Lima, and at Tiahuanaco, more than 10,000 feet above sea level in the Andes, near Lake Titicaca in Bolivia. Local legend says Tiahuanaco, with its huge Gateway of the Sun and impressive remains of temples, was already in ruins when the Inca empire reached its zenith. Modern research confirms the mysterious civilization that built it predates the Incas by several centuries.

But Manco's stronghold of Vilcabamba continued to elude both bounty hunters and archaeologists alike. The American Hiram Bingham thought he had traced it in 1911 on a mountaintop west of Cuzco, smothered under years of jungle growth, at a site known as Machu Picchu. Its buildings and terraces are remarkably preserved, but Bingham found little else in the way of Inca treasure. Now, archaeologists think, the true Vilcabamba may be on another site, several miles from Machu Picchu and even more inaccessible.

The 19th-century craze for hunting lost cities in former Spanish America was not confined to Inca territories, however. In two years from 1839, two young explorers found traces of no fewer than five ruined cities in and around the Yucatán peninsula – posing the riddle of the mysterious Maya which is still not fully solved.

ABOVE Machu Picchu, high in the Andes, was thought to be the fabled last stronghold of the Inca when its overgrown but magnificent remains were rediscovered in 1911. Now, experts have their doubts.

THE MYSTERIOUS MAYA

BELOW This stela, or carved stone, found in Guatemala depicts a human sacrifice. The victims of such bloody rites were usually captives taken in wars between rival Mayan cities.

LEFT Soaring flights of stairs are a feature of monuments in rediscovered Maya cities such as Uxmal, Mexico. Maya pyramids occasionally contain burials, but they are primarily platforms for temples.

LEFT The Mayan sun god is shown on an intricately carved stela from Guatemala. Collectors pay a fortune for these relics, but trade in them is being banned.

he Aztec and Inca empires ransacked by Spanish conquistadors were two of the three greatest civilizations to flourish in pre-Columbian America. The Maya, the third and perhaps greatest of all, was already in sharp decline when the Spanish arrived. As a result, its achievements were largely unrecognized until the middle of the 19th century, when two young explorers, an American and an Englishman, joined forces to investigate legends of lost cities in Central America.

John Lloyd Stephens, the American, was a lawyer and amateur antiquary who had already traveled widely in Asia. His English partner, Frederick Catherwood, was a talented artist. Together, between 1839 and 1842, they braved rain forests, an inhospitable climate, and sometimes hostile natives of the Yucatán peninsula and surrounding areas to test the truth of the stories for themselves. What they found, with the help of local Indians, surpassed their wildest expectations – huge stone pyramids, temples and palaces, monuments, and statues in the green grip of the jungle. Many were decorated with ornate and complex carvings and some with hieroglyphic writing.

Altogether, the pair discovered four cities or religious ceremonial sites of the Maya, whose civilization developed from about 2000 BC and reached its height from AD 300 to AD 900 – Copán in Honduras, Quiriga in Guatemala, Palenque and Uxmal in Mexico. A fifth, Chichén Itzá in Mexico, was partly Maya, but, it is now thought, was mainly built by the warrior Toltecs who flourished briefly as the Maya declined.

Catherwood's romantic drawings helped to make these and subsequently discovered Maya sites of Central America a magnet for archaeologists and treasure hunters alike. The battle between the two

is still going on in the region, sometimes involving arms; teams of local looters were shown robbing previously unknown grave complexes in a British television film screened in 1990.

The main targets of the grave-robbers are artifacts in jade, the most precious material known to the Maya, such as the magnificent 7th-century death mask of Pacal, a ruler of Palenque. But decorated items in dark, glass-like obsidian fetch a high price among collectors. So do ceramics so long as they are covered with Mayan hieroglyphs; a single plate can bring between $4,000 and $6,000 at auction. Superbly carved stone slabs, called *stelae*, are less in demand since the United States passed laws against trade in them.

The activities of the plunderers, mostly poor subsistence farmers, has put archaeologists in a race against time to find out all they can about the Maya. In particular, they want to know what caused the relatively sudden collapse of the only truly literate pre-Columbian civilization.

RIGHT The Mayan/Toltec city of Chichén Itzá, Mexico, is one of five rediscovered by Stephens and Catherwood in 1839–42. This domed building has been named "The Observatory": the Maya were experts in astronomy.

WELL OF BLOOD

The scale and grandeur of the rediscovered cities of the Maya, their hieroglyphic writing system, and the complex calendar they evolved all combine to persuade some people that Mayan development must have been influenced by a mysterious external force. At the beginning of this century, a New Englander called Edward Thompson convinced himself that the Maya ruins could be connected with the myth of the lost continent of Atlantis, and traveled to Mexico with the backing of the Peabody Museum at Harvard to test his theories on the spot.

As it happened, Thompson quickly discarded any thoughts of an Atlantean connection, and settled down at the Maya/Toltec center of Chichén Itzá on the Yucatán peninsula to investigate a local legend. According to that, a ceremonial well near the main temples had once been used for human sacrifices.

With the aid of a mechanical scoop and local helpers, Thompson probed the depths of the great well – at the top it is nearly 200 feet across. At first, he found nothing extraordinary. But then, amid the sludge, artifacts began to appear, among them a spear holder. Further dredging yielded several small gold bells, jewelry, and bones subsequently identified as human. Eagerly, Thompson procured a diving suit and descended into the well. He found dozens more gold items.

The priceless collection was smuggled out of Mexico and back to Harvard, leading to a long-running legal battle over the ownership. Subsequently, part was returned to the Mexican authorities, who then took on the task of well-dredging

LEFT The Maya were the only truly literate civilization of pre-Columbian America. Their hieroglyphs carved on stone are relatively commonplace, but few of their manuscripts survive. Those that do are priceless.

themselves. At the most recent count, some 4,000 artifacts have been recovered.

However, unlike the Aztec and Inca, the Maya seem generally to have worked little in gold. Jade and obsidian are thought to have been their most precious commodities, and the relatively few gold items found in late Mayan graves are said to be of Aztec origin. The Aztecs, whose bloodthirsty religious rites required a constant stream of human sacrifices, eventually overran the Toltecs, who in turn are believed to have superseded the Maya at Chichén Itzá.

Translation of the Mayan hieroglyphs is helping to shed light on the complex relationships between these various Central American civilizations. The code of the glyphs had not been cracked in Thompson's day, and it is only since the late 1950s that real progress has been made in deciphering them and piecing together the Maya story – a progress hampered by the

RIGHT *In this carving from a Mayan building, a priest cuts his tongue with a rope while kneeling before a god. The Mayan religion was bloodthirsty, though evidently less so than that of the Aztecs. That was based on constant human sacrifice.*

ABOVE *Intricately worked jade was precious to the Maya. This example shows a seated dignitary, and dates from about AD 900. It was excavated at Las Cuevas in Belize.*

continuing loss of inscribed artifacts to treasure hunters. The mysteries of the Mayan calendar have now been unraveled, too. It is based on five interconnected cycles (against the three of day, month, and year we mostly use), with a starting point corresponding to August 13, 3114 BC in the Western calendar.

The biggest breakthrough yet in understanding the Maya, however, may come from the discovery, near San Salvador, of an entire village buried suddenly in a volcanic eruption about 600 AD, like a Central American Pompeii. The site has not yielded treasure in the conventional sense, but artifacts so far recovered include the oldest of only five known Mayan hieroglyphic books. In 1989, it was sent to the Smithsonian for study.

LEFT *The façades of Mayan buildings in the abandoned city of Uxmal are intricately sculpted. In its heyday, Uxmal may have had a population of up to 50,000.*

KING SOLOMON'S MINES

RIGHT English author Sir Henry Rider Haggard (1856–1925) blended fact, fiction, and, seemingly, futurology in his African adventure tale King Solomon's Mines.

Allan Quatermain recalls: "There we stood and shrieked with laughter over the gems which were ours, which had been found for *us* thousands of years ago by the patient delvers in the great hole yonder, and stored for *us* by Solomon's long-dead overseer . . . millions of pounds' worth of diamonds, and thousands of pounds' worth of gold and ivory."

Quatermain, of course, exists only as the fictitious hero of H. Rider Haggard's 1885 African adventure novel *King Solomon's Mines*. But at the time Haggard was writing it, Africa and diamonds were very topical subjects, and his book both reflected previous events and curiously foreshadowed some to come.

The vast Kimberley diamond mines in South Africa had been discovered less than 20 years earlier. The empire-building Englishman Cecil Rhodes had made a fortune from them. More or less as Haggard put pen to paper, the insatiable Rhodes was looking north from Cape Colony to the lands of what is now Zimbabwe, hoping to secure new mineral rights and further wealth.

The territory Rhodes had his eye on, and eventually annexed, was then uncolonized by Europeans. It was dominated by the native empire of the Matabele and ruled from Bulawayo by King Lobengula. Returning travelers told tales of its many huge and mysterious stone ruins and long-abandoned gold mines. These Haggard stirred into his fictional brew.

Rhodes won his mining concessions from Lobengula, moved into the area, and became fascinated by the most impressive of the ruined sites – Great Zimbabwe, from which the modern state takes its name. Its complex construction was held by Rhodes and others of that epoch to be beyond the capabilities of local Africans. Rhodes himself favored the theory that Great Zimbabwe had been the Biblical city of Ophir, renowned for its gold and precious stones, especially during the reign of King Solomon.

A preliminary investigation of Great Zimbabwe in 1891 revealed nothing to

LEFT The stone tower and wall of the enclosure in the ruins of Great Zimbabwe.

confirm that idea. Then Rhodes and Lobengula fell out. The empire builder's private army defeated the Matabele, driving them out of their lands. Lobengula fled from Bulawayo in 1893, supposedly taking with him personal treasure of diamonds, ivory, and gold worth an estimated $14 million – an uncanny echo of what Haggard had described in his earlier novel.

With the Matabele no longer a force, Europeans were free to seek the ancient treasure they thought should lie around the ruined sites. For reasons of his own, Rhodes would not allow excavations at Great Zimbabwe itself. But at Dhlo Dhlo a profusion of gold ornaments together weighing some 80 pounds were found, and smaller hauls came from other sites. At one of them, Mundie, two skeletons were unearthed draped in gold jewelry. There was also ample evidence of worked-out gold mines, which, it was said, had once produced 300 tons of the precious metal.

Presumably, Rhodes held high hopes for his "Ophir" of Great Zimbabwe. However, he died in 1902. Excavations of that year revealed only a few gold items, and little more conventional "treasure" has been found since. Subsequent archaeological studies show that Great Zimbabwe and the other sites were the products of local African cultures, probably around the time of the Middle Ages in Europe. The much older, Biblical Ophir is now thought to have been in Arabia, not Africa.

There remains the mystery of Lobengula's treasure, reputedly hidden in a cave somewhere near the upper reaches of the Zambesi River. An expedition in the 1920s failed to find it – but then it did not have Haggard's hero Allan Quatermain as a member.

ABOVE An aerial view of the ancient city of Great Zimbabwe, showing the great enclosure. Cecil Rhodes believed this was the source of King Solomon's vast wealth.

4 : TO WORLDS BEYOND

Many civilizations in many ages have sent their notables to the grave with goods reflecting their status in this life, and to meet their supposed needs in a world beyond. This custom has preserved for us some of the most magnificent ancient treasures ever found.

Best known are the riches from the tomb of the Egyptian ruler Tutankhamun, whose solid gold, jewel-bedecked coffin alone weighed almost 300 pounds. But there are many others, from the jade suits of Chinese emperors to the golden jewelry and accoutrements of a mighty Saxon leader.

All could be overshadowed, however, by treasures now emerging from the last resting places of the queens of Assyria, in modern-day Iraq. Archaeologists have braved a 2,700-year-old curse to unearth the stupendous collections of worked gold the tombs contain.

TREASURES OF THE BOY-PHARAOH

BELOW Tutankhamun's stunning treasures lay hidden beneath the hills at Thebes for 3,300 years, until Howard Carter (second from left and left in the insets) revealed them after a search lasting two decades.

The Valley of the Kings at Thebes in Egypt is a small, dry, dusty canyon on the west bank of the River Nile. There is little about its outward appearance to suggest it would yield one of the most stunning archaeological finds of all time – nearly 2,000 fabulous items, many of gold, from the tomb of the boy-king Tutankhamun.

So vast is this 3,300-year-old treasure that its value is incalculable. It took five years to remove from the site, and another five to catalogue. Even now, some 70 years after it was found, experts have still not completed full descriptions of each magnificent object.

The discovery of Tutankhamun's resting place is a monument to the patience and persistence of the British archaeologist Howard Carter. For the best part of 20 years, he was engaged in excavations in the valley, the burial place of 62 rulers and high dignitaries of ancient Egypt's New Kingdom between about 1550 and 1070 BC.

According to Egyptian custom of that period, the mummified bodies of dead pharaohs were interred in tombs hardly marked on the outside. Inside, however,

OPPOSITE PAGE The 2,000 items recovered from Tutankhamun's tomb defy description or valuation. They are simply without parallel in the annals of Egyptian archaeology.

it was a different story. The mummies were surrounded by huge displays of precious grave goods, reflecting the status and prestige of the rulers in life and, perhaps, their likely needs in the world to come. The choice of the little-used valley as a royal cemetery and the lack of outward display were intended to protect the lavish contents of the tombs from the attentions of grave robbers. However, by Carter's time the known tombs had long since been ransacked.

At first, Carter was a member of an archaeological team headed by the American Theodore M. Davis. Over several years from 1902, Davis and his colleagues tracked down a number of previously unknown tombs. They recovered some rich funeral objects, but mostly these graves, like the others, had been raided. Eventually, Davis, who was dying, gave up, convinced the valley had no more to offer. Carter soldiered on, with financial backing from a British patron, Lord Carnarvon. For six fruitless years, he surveyed and dug – and found nothing. By 1922, Carter and Carnarvon were ready to call it a day. They agreed it would be their last excavation season, as only a small area of the central valley floor remained unexplored.

The breakthrough came soon after daybreak on November 4, 1922. Carter's workmen discovered a flight of steps leading downward, below the already known tomb of the pharaoh Ramesses IV. Quickly, Carter ordered the steps cleared, to reveal a door bearing the seals of the necropolis guards. A lesser man might have pressed on there and then. But Carter cabled to Lord Carnarvon in England and waited on tenterhooks for almost three weeks until his patron could arrive on site. The day after Carnarvon arrived, he discovered the seal with Tutankhamun's name on it. Only then was the door opened, onto a passage leading to another door. Carter made a small hole in that, held a light to it, and squinted in. Eagerly, Lord Carnarvon asked him what he saw. Carter just gasped . . . "Wonderful things!"

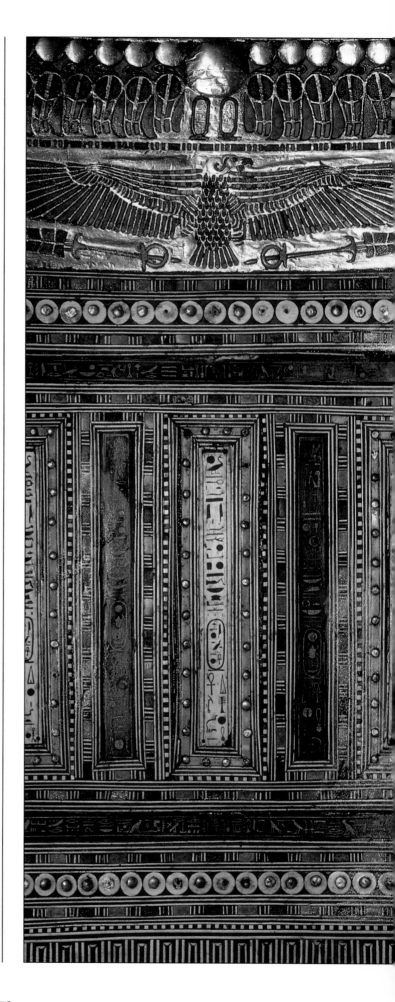

WHO WAS TUTANKHAMUN?

ABOVE The breathtaking death-mask of Tutankhamun rested on the shoulders of his mummified corpse. It was made from beaten gold, inlaid with lapis lazuli and obsidian, and intricately worked.

depictions of a vulture and a cobra, representing Tutankhamun's authority over Upper and Lower Egypt. The mummy was encased in a solid gold and bejeweled coffin weighing almost 300 pounds, inside two outer wooden coffins covered with gold leaf and gilt, respectively. Those in turn were encased in a quartzite sarcophagus, protected by a series of gilded shrines.

Painstaking and professional, Carter took some four months before he was ready to breach this inner sanctum. There was plenty to occupy his attention in the outer rooms – including four dismantled chariots of gilded wood, a gilded and inlaid throne with paneling depicting the sumptuous life of an Egyptian pharaoh, superb jewelry, alabaster vases, gilded couches, inlaid chests and gaming boards, and ostrich-feather fans.

Carter's laconic first description of Tutankhamun's treasure ranks high in any list of British understatements. The entire four-chamber tomb proved to be packed with precious objects overwhelming in their magnificence. Its dry air ensured that even wood and wickerwork had survived three millennia intact.

At the heart of the burial complex lay Tutankhamun's mummy, its face clad in a death mask of beaten gold inlaid with semiprecious stones. Its brow bears

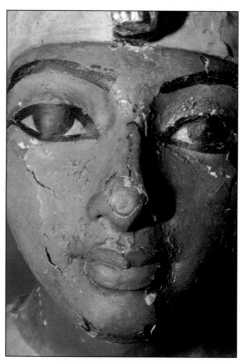

LEFT A decorated wooden effigy of the Egyptian boy-king is almost painfully lifelike, apart from the eyes. It contrasts strikingly with the opulent formality of the death-mask.

RIGHT The sensuous golden figure of a goddess stands in a richly carved shrine taken from Tutankhamun's tomb in the Valley of the Kings, Egypt.

The wooden and gilded statues Carter found are breathtaking in their craftsmanship and attention to detail. One of Selket, a scorpion goddess, depicts her in a clinging, sheer linen robe as erotic today as it must have been more than 3,000 years ago. Another, of the jackal-god Anubis, captures the bone and muscle beneath flanks that almost seem to quiver.

Ironically and despite all this magnificence, we now know that Tutankhamun was a relatively insignificant figure among the pharaohs of ancient Egypt. He came to the throne at the age of only nine or ten and died in 1325 BC at the age of 18 or 19, possibly violently. His very obscurity protected his tomb from grave-robbers,

though there is evidence that it was opened and resealed possibly twice after the burial. But if such splendor could be lavished on a minor monarch, we can only wonder at what more important rulers must have taken with them to their tombs in the Valley of the Kings.

According to popular belief, the pharaohs left behind them a curse to bring misfortune on anyone disturbing their remains. Although this idea was put about by a British Gothic novelist called Marie Corelli, Lord Carnarvon's death shortly after Tutankhamun's tomb was opened helped to spread it. In fact, Carnarvon died from an infected insect bite. Carter lived for another 17 years.

FICKLE JADE

ard, translucent jade varying in color from shades of green to near-white held mystical properties for many ancient peoples all over the world. In China, it has been revered for more than 3,000 years, and only in recent times has gold come to outrank jade as a precious commodity among the Chinese.

The native peoples of North America regarded jade as a protector against snake-bite, and in Central America the Maya valued it highly. In medieval Europe, it was believed to cure stomach disorders. The Chinese went further, associating jade with immortality and the protection of the body against decay after death. This belief led to the creation of some of the most spectacular artifacts ever fashioned for ancient rulers – whole body suits and masks of jade and gold to encase their corpses at burial.

Like the Egyptians, the Chinese for many centuries interred their dignitaries with

BELOW Only powerful rulers in ancient China, and their consorts, could afford to go to their graves in suits and death-masks of precious jade. This restored example comes from the tomb of Princess Tan Lian, who died in the late 2nd century BC.

precious and everyday objects for use in the afterlife, sometimes in huge quantities. As in Egypt, grave robbers subsequently ransacked many of the tombs, not least for jade. In one notable's grave, modern investigators have found the body of a robber who died or was killed in the course of his crime.

When units of the Chinese Army were carrying out construction work in 1968 at Mancheng, about 70 miles southwest of Peking, they uncovered in a hillside the entrance to an artificial cave. Archaeologists summoned to the site to investigate discovered within it two undisturbed burial chambers, filled with several thousand priceless artifacts in jade, bronze, and ceramic. Most intriguing of all, however, were the heaps of jade disks intermingled with human remains – all that was left of the jade suits and the bodies they were confidently expected to preserve.

Careful analysis and reconstruction showed there were two corpses, of a man and a woman. The woman's suit was about 5½ feet long; it and the death mask were made up of 2,160 pieces of jade. The man's suit was more than 6 feet long, with 2,690 disks of the precious stone. Each magnificent suit had been held together with gold wire – more than 1 pound for the woman and 2.5 pounds for the man. Each would have represented a fortune in its day, and is beyond price now.

The male corpse was identified as that of Prince Liu Sheng, son of the Emperor

Jingdi of the Han dynasty of Chinese rulers, who died in about 113 BC. The woman was Princess Dou Wan, Liu's principal wife, who died about 12 years before he did.

Since the Mancheng finds, newly discovered tombs of other Chinese notables have been yielding a stream of treasures. From the grave of the Emperor Wendi, north of Canton, came another jade suit, a collection of more than 40 carved ritual swords in jade, and items in silver and ivory. Wendi did not go to his tomb alone; ten servants or concubines had been killed to accompany him in the afterlife, in a gruesome custom many Chinese rulers observed. One, in the time of the Shang dynasty around 1200 BC, was buried with 48 subjects, all beheaded for the funeral by a ritual axe decorated with a menacing, leering face.

Prince Zheng, named Shihuangdi or "first emperor," evidently did not subscribe to the practice, though in life he did not shirk from bloodshed to unite China under his rule. When he was buried in the 3rd century BC, the man who built the Great Wall had as companions in death the 6,000-7,000 members of a unique, life-sized terracotta army. This masterpiece of craftsmanship was uncovered at Mount Lishan in the Yellow River valley from 1974.

One of the richest and most revealing Chinese tombs so far found did not belong to an emperor or warrior – but to a middle-aged woman whose death 2,000 years ago was probably due to gallstones.

ABOVE and OPPOSITE Dragon pendants in elaborately worked jade which date from the 3rd or 4th century BC. In this period – the late Chou (Zhou) Dynasty – China was a seething mass of warring states.

BELOW A pair of gilded bronze leopards from the tomb of Princess Dou Wan. Little remained of Dou Wan's body, 2,000 years after her death, but her priceless jade burial suit did survive.

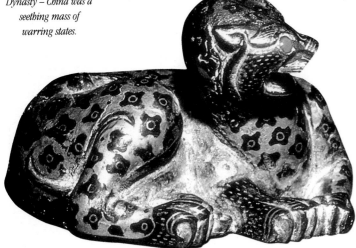

LACQUER FOR A LADY

Richly colored Chinese lacquerware is highly prized today, as it was 2,100 years ago by the luxury-loving rich and powerful of China under the Han dynasty of emperors. At that time, techniques for producing lacquerware by coating wooden or fabric objects with the resin from the lacquer tree improved to a point where they have hardly been bettered. The revival of Chinese archaeology since the 1920s has yielded many examples, but none so spectacular or well-preserved as those found in the tomb of a wealthy lady at Mawangdui in what was the principality of Changsha.

The main chamber of the tomb lay some 60 feet down in the earth, below a mound and pit packed with soil. The chamber itself was surrounded with clay and charcoal, an arrangement ensuring that artifacts inside were preserved in near-perfect condition through two millenia.

For extra preservation, the body itself was clad, not in a jade suit, but in layers and layers of ordinary, though sumptuous,

BELOW Ladies of a Chinese court are painted on silk in this contemporary portrait. Bronze mirrors and other articles like those they are shown carrying were found in profusion at Mawangdui.

ABOVE *A rich red and black bowl is just one of 184 pieces of 2,000-year-old Chinese lacquerware from the Lady of Changsha's tomb. It is the most magnificent assembly of lacquer of its period yet found.*

screens, trays, boxes, vases, cups, and plates in rich red and black designs.

The modern equivalent of the woman's wardrobe for the afterworld would cost a fortune. There are silk robes, dresses, and other garments, some crammed into bamboo cases which occupied an entire side of the tomb chamber, and rolls and rolls of silk fabric. Touchingly, there are four pairs of tiny silk shoes with tie-ribbons. More silk draped the innermost coffin, in the form of a beautiful painted banner depicting paradise and the underworld.

As befitted an accomplished wife of her times, the Lady of Changsha was evidently a musician. The tomb contained a stringed instrument resembling a zither, and pipes. There are bamboo mats and fans, mirrors of polished bronze, and dozens of small wooden figures, including musicians and dancers in silk costumes – even medicinal herbs and the remains of food such as rice, fish, and chicken.

clothing, and placed in the innermost of four richly decorated coffins. So successfully did this work that archaeologists found the woman's skin still nearly as supple as it had been in life. Medical experts could determine that she had suffered, among other disorders, from anemia and chronic gallstones. Those probably brought on a heart attack which killed her sometime about 150 BC, when she was around the age of 50.

The woman is thought to have been the wife of a top-ranking official in Changsha. Certainly, the magnificent goods that went with her to the grave indicate substantial wealth. The lacquerware collection alone is superb – nearly 200 items including

Amazingly, the excavators found the tomb contained a full inventory of its contents, on a stack of bamboo pads crammed in among the lacquerware, wooden figures, and a collection of tiny tin bells. There are more than 300 of these pads, as further witness of the splendor in which the Chinese ruling classes lived – and died – shortly before the time of Christ.

LEFT *The tomb at Mawangdui contained four coffins, set one inside each other – an arrangement that helped preserve the body in its near-original state. The three inner coffins are intricately decorated, and the innermost is lined with silk.*

HORSEMEN OF THE STEPPES

or 1,000 years or so before the birth of Christ and several centuries afterward, the open steppes north of the Black Sea and the Caucasus were the roaming ground of a succession of war-like, nomadic tribes. Their way of life was bloodthirsty, but they left a legacy of magnificent artifacts, combining cruelty with beauty, that established an artistic tradition throughout most of Europe.

The Scythians buried their chieftains on the open steppe in mound graves called *kurganii*, with all the trappings of their earthly status. Many of these tombs were subsequently plundered. From those overlooked by robbers, modern archaeologists have recovered superb brooches, plaques, shields, vases, and other items.

At the western and southern fringes of their territory, the Scythians traded with the Greeks, and some treasures found are

Among the first of these peoples were the Cimmerians and the related Thracians, whose goldwork has been found in large quantities in modern-day Bulgaria. About 800 BC, the Cimmerians were driven from the Black Sea lands by the warrior-horsemen of the Scythians, who in turn were superseded by the Sarmatians.

ABOVE RIGHT A mythical winged griffin and other, real-life beasts appear on the flanks of a Scythian gold stag, now in the Hermitage Museum, Leningrad, U.S.S.R.

of Greek origin, such as the gold Solokha comb, which carries a finely worked and extremely detailed hunting scene. But native Scythian craftsmen were lavish, too, in their use of gold and, when the opportunity arose, electrum. That is a naturally occurring alloy of gold and silver from which the earliest known forerunners of

ABOVE Scythian warriors are depicted on a vase found in a burial mound of the 4th century BC in the Crimea. The vase is made from the precious natural alloy electrum. Its style shows Greek influence.

be a ceremony of blood brotherhood. A later brooch, Sarmatian rather than Scythian and from Maikop in the Caucasus, gorily shows a warrior brandishing the severed head of an enemy.

The animal symbolism of the Scythians unquestionably influenced the art of the Celts, who spread it westward through Europe. Warriors' tombs at Pazaryk in Siberia show it was rife further eastward in the Scythian era, too. There, the bodies of several nomadic horsemen were buried, in about 400 BC together with the steeds that had served them in life, complete with saddles and bridles. The tombs were later ransacked for precious objects, and the robbers left holes through which rain entered and froze.

modern coins were also fashioned, around 650 BC in Lydia in what is now eastern Turkey.

Working with such precious metals, the Scythians developed a distinctive form of decoration in which animals play a prominent part; they are much more stylized than the realistic-looking beasts created by the Greeks. Sometimes the animals were depicted alone, as, for example, the splendid carved gold stag recovered from a 6-7th-century BC *kurgan* at Kostromskaya in the Kuban, south Russia. Often, they were used to decorate more practical objects such as weapons and armor, horse-trappings, and vases. A shield recovered from a *kurgan* at Kul Oba in the Crimea, for instance, carries a panther.

Other themes reflect the warlike customs of the Scythians. A gold plaque, also from Kul Oba, shows two warriors drinking from the same horn in what seems to

2,000 YEAR OLD TATTOO

When the graves were rediscovered in the 1920s, the bodies and remaining grave goods had been remarkably preserved by the ice. One mummified corpse, presumed to be the chieftain, was extensively tattooed with animal themes – deer, wild goats, and fabulous monsters including a griffin. Similar designs appeared on the brightly colored wall hangings and carpets the robbers had left in the tombs.

TWILIGHT OF THE CELTS

ike the Scythians, the Celts were a warrior race. From about 650 BC until their conquest by the Romans, they dominated much of central and western Europe. Part of their success was due to their skill in ironworking, then in its infancy. They hammered iron into short, stabbing swords and, on occasion, fittings for their chariots. But they also delighted in decoration – animal themes more stylized even than those of the Scythians, and riotous swirling patterns of curves and circles almost modern in their abstract designs.

For decorative items, the Celts worked not only in iron, but also in bronze, gold, silver, and electrum. Sometimes, colored glass or semiprecious stones were added to give the final touch of luxury. Celtic artifacts that have survived are among the richest treasures of pre-Roman Europe.

The Celts were not one tribe, but many, with groups of local chieftains ruled over by regional kings. So their customs could vary. Nevertheless, important figures seem generally to have been buried with a wide variety of grave goods, while even the less important took their personal jewelry to the tomb.

At Lexden near Colchester in England, for example, the grave of a local Iron Age aristocrat contained silver-studded chain mail, gold-embroidered cloth, ears of wheat in silver, and bronze statues of beasts such as bulls and boars. At Vix in France, the resting-place of a Celtic princess yielded bronze statues, a huge bronze urn, a gold diadem, and other jewelry. In Yorkshire, England, several graves have been found containing the remains of

LEFT Circular designs on the Battersea Shield are typical of the Celtic decorative style. The bronze shield was found in the River Thames at Battersea, London. It may have been a votive offering to a Celtic god in or after the 2nd century BC.

war-chariots. Most such tombs are of men, but one is said to have contained the skeleton of a sturdy woman – perhaps a forebear of Queen Boadicea (Boudicca), who led a revolt against the Romans occupying Britain in the 1st century AD.

Such chariot burials in England do not normally contain the occupant's horses. But in one near Market Weighton the remains of a pair of small ponies were unearthed. A superb, stylized horse mask in bronze, found at Stanwick in Yorkshire, may have been an artistic substitute for the real thing.

Pools and rivers seem to have played an important part in the religious rites of the Celts, and some of the most spectacular examples of Celtic craftsmanship in bronze have been recovered from water – though from this distance in time it is impossible to know whether they were thrown in deliberately as part of a ritual, or dropped accidentally. The River Thames in London, for instance, has yielded a horned chieftain's helmet with delicate plant-like decorations, and an impressive golden-bronze shield with red glass and enamel trimming and elaborate circular designs in relief.

The apogee of the Celtic metalworkers' art in Britain, however, was reached with torcs – beautiful bands they forged for the necks of senior chieftains. One hoard alone, found in Snettisham in Norfolk, must have been worth a king's ransom even in its day.

BELOW A Celtic chariot-burial at Arras Barrow, Yorkshire, England, contained the skeleton of a woman with some of her possessions, including harness trappings of bronze and an iron mirror.

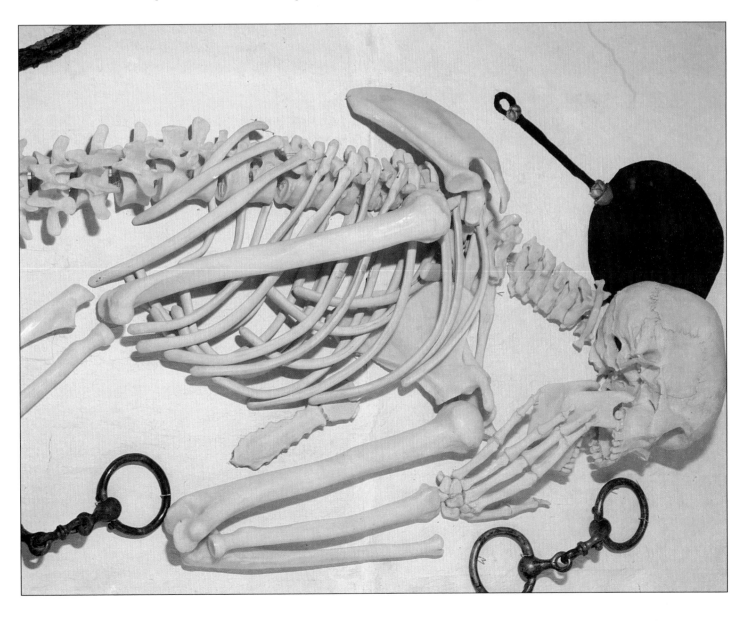

SHIP BURIAL AT SUTTON HOO

ABOVE Gold coins from Sutton Hoo were minted in mainland Europe. They date the ship burial to after AD 625.

Barrow-digging – plunging into ancient burial mounds in search of antique treasures and curios – was almost a Sunday sport for rich landowners 200 years ago or so. It was practiced in much of Europe and in the United States, and mostly it was an unscientific and haphazard business. Masses of valuable archaeological evidence and countless relics of long-established cultures were destroyed for

RIGHT The shape of the Sutton Hoo burial ship was almost perfectly preserved in its sandy tomb. The treasure it contained is the most magnificent legacy of Dark Age Britain.

the diversion of the well-to-do. So it is little short of a miracle that the most magnificent Dark Age treasure ever found in Britain – some say the most magnificent of any epoch – should have escaped the process unscathed.

A cluster of grassy mounds overlooking the estuary of the River Deben at Sutton Hoo near Woodbridge in Suffolk seems to have been tampered with in this way.

But faced with the sweaty task of hacking into 15 barrows, the diggers evidently gave up before desecrating all of them. When in 1938 the owner of the land, Mrs. Edith Pretty, gave an amateur archaeologist and his helpers permission to investigate the mounds, some were more or less intact.

The first three barrows opened produced evidence of the barrow-diggers' depredations and a few relics. They were unspectacular, but confirmed that the mounds dated from the Dark Ages, the period in England between the last days of Roman occupation in the late 5th century AD and about AD 1000, of which historical knowledge is patchy. Sometime early in that era, the real prototype for the legendary King Arthur of Camelot is thought to have flourished.

Then, entering the largest mound, the amazed modern investigators were confronted with an undisturbed line of rusted nails and a few fragments of wood in the sand. These were the last vestiges of a large ship, of a kind used by the Saxons who invaded Britain as the Romans left, and whom the real-life Arthur fought.

So important was this find that professional archaeologists from the British Museum were called in. By then, it was

BELOW Garnets and glass add color to the intricately worked gold purse-lid. The purse was worn on a belt around the waist of a Saxon leader.

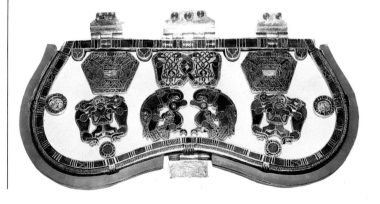

RIGHT Experts have painstakingly reconstructed an awe-inspiring bronze and iron war-helmet from surviving fragments. Only kings owned such headgear in Saxon times.

iron goods, weaponry, and armor, including fragments of a fearsome, gilded war helmet decorated with a dragon design and probably made in Scandinavia. There were the remnants of ceremonial clothes.

Above all, there was gold, richly worked in intricate patterns and trimmed, in some pieces, with semiprecious garnets, colored glass, and enamel. The belt buckle alone is 5 inches long and weighs 14 ounces, in solid pale gold decorated with snakes. There are gold clasps and a gold sword hilt. Finest of all is a gold purse lid, with figures of animals, birds, and men, and three gold hinges which originally attached it to a belt. Around this, the archaeologists found some 30 gold coins and small ingots, dating from about AD 625.

But perhaps the most significant of all finds at Sutton Hoo are an iron standard with the bronze figure of a stag and a stone staff that could be a scepter, both emblems of rank and power. These give the clue that the man honored in the mound was almost certainly a royal figure. Whatever his precise identity, he has left a wealth of treasures for posterity to admire.

ABOVE The solid gold belt-buckle was probably made in England, but, like the war-helmet, is Scandinavian in style. It would have been worn on ceremonial occasions.

1939 and Britain was on the eve of the Second World War. The professional team had to work fast, recovering what they could before the site was filled in and the land above used as a military tank range. After the war, the mound was re-excavated to round out knowledge of its purpose. As late as 1989, experts were still arguing about some of the details. But the general picture is clear.

This was the funeral memorial of a mighty Saxon leader – possibly Raedwald, King of East Anglia and High King of England in the 7th century AD. It was a stupendous tribute to a dead aristocrat.

The ship, reconstructed as a plaster cast, formed a sort of massive outer coffin. It was nearly 90 feet long and 14 feet wide, without a deck, and would have needed up to 40 people to row it. There is dispute about whether it actually put to sea or was purely for funeral purposes. But it had been dragged nearly one-third of a mile from the waters of the Deben. Amidships, the investigators found traces of a wooden cabin piled high with priceless treasures to accompany the king to the afterlife.

The array was phenomenal. There were silver bowls, dishes, plates, and a great tureen, some imported from the eastern fringes of the Roman Empire. There were

BELOW A rich, stylized figure of a bird added a decorative touch to a Saxon shield in the 7th century AD.

GODS OF THE OLMECS

*D*aily life must have been a round of terror for the Olmec, whose culture rose and fell between 1200 and 400 BC in what are now the states of Veracruz and Tabasco on Mexico's Gulf coast. They worshiped a fearsome array of gods who seem to have been part-human, part-animal, and whose displeasure could wreak havoc at any time.

These deities were based on local creatures such as snakes, armadilloes, eagles, and caymans, or tropical alligators. The most powerful of all was the jaguar-god, a snarling creature with a thick-lipped, fanged mouth. Among other things, he was responsible for rain.

To placate these vengeful beings, the Olmec religion required humans to make votive offerings to them – gifts of precious items deposited in special places on special occasions, such as perhaps a birth or a funeral. These religious rites helped to preserve for posterity some of the finest artifacts of the early Americas.

For the Olmec had a highly developed trade network with neighboring peoples, through which they obtained materials such as glass-like obsidian, jade, and green-black serpentine. Using these and other decorative stone found locally, the Olmec carved their offerings to the gods, some in exquisite detail.

In the later period of Olmec civilization, the most important center was La Venta. It incorporated a complex religious shrine which, some experts believe, was laid out to represent the stylized head of a jaguar.

In the shrine itself, there are serpentine pavements depicting jaguars and a 100-foot earth pyramid which would have taken 800 men three years to build.

One of the best-preserved collections of votive offerings was discovered at La Venta, in a pit filled with different colored sands. More than a dozen carved figures of serpentine, granite, and jade were clustered around six axe-like objects known to archaeologists as *celts*, exactly as they had been positioned about 2,500 years ago.

These votive figures are of humans, and are relatively crude. However, from burial sites and elsewhere, investigators have recovered other offerings that demonstrate the artistic skills of the Olmec at their height. One priceless, highly worked celt in jade, a little over 10 inches long, depicts the human face of the jaguar-god in great detail. Its curled lips make the face too cruel-looking to be described as beautiful, and even today it exerts a powerful effect.

Another figure, in serpentine, shows the same god in jaguar form, but upright. Its eyes are of glistening pyrite (fool's gold). Altogether more pleasant is a pottery armadillo grave object, quite lifelike and polished to a warm reddish hue.

The Olmec gods were the forerunners of those worshipped by later Central American civilizations such as the Aztec, whose religious rites did not require just votive objects, but the wholesale slaughter of human victims, mostly prisoners taken from neighboring peoples.

RIGHT The ancient peoples of Central America made ceremonial masks from jade fragments laid as a mosaic on a wooden frame. Shells and obsidian were often used for the eyes.

CURSE OF A GOLDEN QUEEN

*T*he stone tablet found by Iraqi archaeologists in 1989 at the entrance to an ancient tomb bore a chilling message: "Whoever in future ... breaks the seals of this grave, up above in the sunlight may his ghost wander thirsting in the open." But archaeologists cannot afford to be superstitious. Ignoring the 2,700-year-old warning, they pressed on – to reveal a magnificent royal burial ground that may eventually prove more plentiful as a source of priceless treasures even than Egypt's Valley of the Kings.

For the tablet was recovered at Nimrud, near Mosul in present-day Iraq and once a major center of the Assyrian empire which at its height in 721-633 BC, stretched from Egypt to the Persian Gulf. The Assyrians were among the cruelest and most rapacious peoples of Old Testament times. Inhabitants of conquered lands were slaughtered wholesale by impaling, decapitation, or flaying, or deported into slavery. The conquerors then looted on the grand scale, especially gold.

Archaeologist Muzahim Mahmud describes the scene as the tomb was opened: "I saw the gold, very bright, mixed with bones and clothes and dust. There was gold from head to toe – many, many pieces." The preliminary tally, according

ABOVE The one-time splendor of the palaces of Nimrud belied the genocidal cruelty of the Assyrian rulers who lived in them. Now the ruins are yielding royal treasures unsurpassed anywhere for scale and beauty. But they carry a curse ...

to *The Times* of London, was more than 80 necklaces, the same number of gold earrings, inlaid gold bracelets, and bowls and other vessels of gold, alabaster, and rock crystal. Owner of this stupendous collection, and invoker of the curse on the tablet, was Yaba, wife of King Tiglath-Pileser III, who seized the Assyrian throne around 744 BC.

Yaba's tomb is far from the whole story, however. Two other royal graves have so far been unearthed under what was once the floor of a palace, and more may be traced. One was reportedly even richer than Yaba's tomb, containing a total of 440 gold items together weighing a staggering 30 pounds. Among these is a gold crown decorated with depictions of pomegranates, grapes, and vine leaves.

Some of the jewelry so far recovered is remarkable in its delicacy. Ear pendants have finely worked flowers or bells and a diadem is of filigree. There could not be a more marked contrast either with the bloodthirstiness of the Assyrians or with the monumental art for which they have hitherto been best known – four-square statues of human-headed bulls and lions,

LEFT Blood-hungry Assyrians rampaged over much of the Middle East 2,700 years ago. This bronze bowl found at Nimrud, showing a lion hunt, may have been booty from an attack on the Phoenicians.

and detailed but stolid relief carvings on limestone slabs.

Ironically, the golden treasures of the palace of Nimrud have narrowly escaped discovery on several previous occasions. Just before 600 BC, the city was sacked by the alliance of Medes and Babylonians which overthrew the Assyrian empire; they missed the underfloor hoards. The remains of the palace were found in the 1840s by the British archaeologist Sir Austen Henry Layard, and then assiduously excavated a century later by another British team. That came within a paving stone's thickness of the tombs. However, it was left to the Iraqis themselves to brave Queen Yaba's curse and to make the finds.

LEFT An Assyrian king of about 850 BC attacks a city, with archers and spearmen. A relief-carving from the North-west Palace at Nimrud.

5: IN TIME

OF WAR

When war threatens, the wise conceal their valuables in a place of safety. Armies on the move have a habit of looting, both on an organized basis to keep their war chests full and as free-enterprise opportunism by soldiers wanting to get rich quick.

Sometimes there is time to evade the looters. During the Saxon invasions of Britain, for example, wealthy civilians evidently managed to bury their most precious possessions before the enemy arrived. Such caches still turn up today.

On other occasions, there is no escape. The Vikings, past masters at the swift seaborne raid, stripped settlements along much of coastal Europe of all the treasure they possessed. Because the Vikings melted most of their booty down, there is no telling what it would be worth now in its original form. The legacy of Viking jewelry made from such spoils is itself magnificent.

The Vikings pall beside the Nazis, who ransacked an entire continent with ruthless efficiency between 1938 and 1945. They carted off gold bullion alone worth $500 billion at a conservative estimate, of which $100 billion has still not been traced.

Then there are the war chests themselves, hidden by armies in flight or simply lost through bad luck. In the first category comes the 500 tons of gold reputedly concealed in Siberia by retreating Tsarist forces. In the second comes the fighting fund of King John of England, which has defied the best efforts of treasure seekers for more than seven centuries.

THE ROMANS IN FLIGHT

At the end of the 4th century AD, the mighty Roman empire was in trouble. Nowhere was the crisis more apparent than in Britain, remote on the northwest fringes of empire. In AD 367, the province was attacked on three sides simultaneously, by Picts from Scotland in the north, by Saxons across the North Sea in the east, and from Irish raiders to the west. Eventually, the Romans regained control, but the damage had been done. On three separate occasions soon afterward, the Roman army protecting Britain left to pursue what it considered to be more immediate matters on the European mainland. On the last occasion, in AD 401, it did not return.

Emboldened by its absence, the barbarians stepped up their onslaughts. Despite strong and prolonged resistance by Romanized British leaders, who probably included the real-life model for King Arthur of legend, waves of Anglo-Saxon invaders from what is now Denmark and Germany surged over the North Sea, eventually to stay.

But even before that, wealthy Romano-British citizens could sense which way the wind blew. They fled from their villas

RIGHT Rich paintings decorated the walls of Roman villas such as the one at Lullingstone in Kent. These were treasures that could not be removed or hidden as Roman Britain faced invasion.

and farms to the safety of towns and then, when those were threatened by the enemy, to who knows where. Buildings abandoned as Roman rule collapsed pay witness to the sumptuous way of life of the rich. The remains of villas such as Lullingstone and farms like that at Chedworth boast elegant mosaic floors, marble columns, and brightly colored frescoes. Dozens of Roman habitations have already been discovered in Britain, and fresh ones are regularly located.

In the 18th century, for example, at Corbridge in Northumberland, a whole collection of Roman silver was collected piecemeal from the River Tyne over a period of 30 years. It included bowls, cups, and vases, and a solid silver wall plaque showing the goddess Minerva and the god Apollo. Probably, all the objects were buried together near the riverbank soon after AD 400, and were gradually released as the bank eroded.

ABOVE The Phoenician princess Europa visited by the god Zeus in the guise of a white bull, from a mosaic floor at Lullingstone Villa.

RIGHT A winged boy rides a dolphin in a mosaic at Fishbourne Palace in southern England. The palace, thought originally to have been built for a local king who collaborated with the Romans, was eventually destroyed by fire.

Richly decorated as they are, however, most yield relatively little in the way of portable treasures. At Lullingstone, for instance, finds include marble busts, copper and tin coins, bronze vessels, and jewelry and glassware – but none of the gold or silver the owner of such a villa might be expected to possess.

Chance discoveries in Britain and throughout Europe provide the probable explanation. Forced to flee, the rich of the Roman epoch took with them any of their most valuable possessions they could and concealed the rest at some considerable distance away from their homes, usually by burying them. This pattern has led to some splendid finds of Roman treasure hoards, entirely by accident.

BELOW A lion devours a deer in a sculpture found at Corbridge, Northumberland, England. Corbridge was an important Roman fort, and has yielded many treasures.

MAGNIFICENT MILDENHALL

ncient silverware, when it has been buried in the earth for centuries, does not keep its shine like gold. It goes dull and grayish black. So when Gordon Butcher, plowing a field at Mildenhall in Suffolk, England, turned up an old tray one day in 1942, he could be forgiven for thinking it was made of non-precious pewter, or possibly lead.

LEFT The boy blowing his conch-shell horn forms the handle to a magnificent silver dish-lid, engraved with both mythical and real-life figures.

RIGHT A perfectly preserved silver platter from Mildenhall shows a satyr and a maenad – male and female participants respectively in the rites of the wine-god Bacchus.

Gordon passed his find to his employer, Sidney Ford, and the pair scanned the freshly plowed soil for other, similar objects. They found them – 33 in all. Sidney collected them up and took them home, where he promptly forgot all about them for the next four years. Only in 1946 were the discoveries reported and the objects properly cleaned.

The cleaning revealed that the items were silver of the highest quality. Further study showed they mostly dated from the 4th century AD, though some were up to 200 years older – suggesting they were the family silver amassed over several generations by wealthy Romans or Romano-Britons. Suffolk, on England's east coast, was in the front line of Saxon invasions of Britain as Roman rule collapsed, so it is assumed the hoard was hidden when the owner fled from a barbarian attack.

The Mildenhall Treasure is one of the most important collections of Roman art yet found in the British Isles. All 34 pieces are highly ornamented and almost per-

BELOW One of four silver ladles turned up by a plowman at Mildenhall. The handles are cast, rather than beaten, in the shape of dolphins – a symbol of social love.

IN TIME OF WAR

fectly preserved. They were made in various places around the Mediterranean and in the Roman province of Gaul, with some that could be British, so the owner could have been a traveled man. A name that fits, though it cannot be proved, is the general Lupicinus, sent by Rome to Britain in the 4th century to stiffen its defenses.

The treasure consists of trays and platters, dishes, goblets, spoons, and finger bowls. The single most magnificent item is a round tray, or salver, measuring 2 feet in diameter. It has a beaded rim, and is decorated with figures of gods and goddesses around a centerpiece depicting the sea god Oceanus.

Round platters show women in flowing robes dancing in abandon. A bowl with a domed lid shows gods and animals, while another has scrollwork leaves and flowers, birds, and rabbits. The four ladles have

LEFT This great salver, or tray, is the single most splendid of the 33 items found at Mildenhall. Such Roman silverware is effectively priceless, but a rock-bottom value of $10 million has been suggested for the entire hoard.

highly decorated handles with silver-gilt dolphins; their eye sockets may once have been filled with precious stones. Some of the spoons carry early Christian markings, and perhaps were given as christening presents.

LEFT The rim of the silver dish is beaded at the outside edge, and chased with complex patterns. The swirled fluting of the bowl itself remains a popular feature for silverware more than 1,500 years after this example was made.

FURY OF THE NORSEMEN

Vikings in swift, deadly longships terrorized the coastal regions of Europe and North Africa between the 8th and 11th centuries AD. From their Scandinavian bases, these intrepid Norsemen sailed westward to America and eastward into Russia.

Sometimes the aims of their voyages were exploration, trade, or settlement. Usually, at least at the beginning of the Viking age, they were for pillage or extortion, practices at which the Vikings were adept. Their lightning sea raids, for example on Lindisfarne Priory on England's northeast coast in AD 793, left the inhabitants little chance to hide their valuables. An 8th-century gold-and-silver chalice found at Armagh in Ireland in 1868 is one of the few examples of treasure possibly concealed to preserve it from Norse raiders.

If booty was not forthcoming immediately, the Vikings would remain, dealing or threatening death, until their victims could buy them off. Using such tactics over a long period of years, they extracted a staggering 685 pounds of gold and 43,042 pounds of silver (detailed in contemporary records) from kings in what is now France. In England, Spain, and North Africa, they extorted what must have been millions of dollars' worth of silver coin. But without a developed monetary system of their own until late in their day, the Vikings had little use for the coinage of others. Neither did they have reverence for the gold and silver objects ripped from Lindisfarne and similar Christian sites that were a favorite target. Much of the coin and plate went into melting pots to make the Vikings' preferred form of wealth – jewelry and other personal items such as sword hilts and horse-trappings that could be ostentatiously displayed, or bartered if the need arose.

Viking chiefs were discouraged from keeping all the spoils for themselves. Court poets exhorted them to be "unfriendly to gold" – that is, to distribute plenty of it as rewards to their followers, for example as rings. Most leaders seem to have obeyed this egalitarian custom.

As a result, though the Vikings have left us a mass of beautiful and priceless artifacts of their own making, few of the original precious objects they looted survive intact. Similarly, Viking treasure caches on the scale of those bequeathed by other warrior peoples or their victims are rare, too.

The biggest cache of Viking gold ever found, on an islet in Ireland's River Shannon, weighed only about 10 pounds. It consisted entirely of decorative armbands, and was unfortunately melted down around the beginning of the 19th century. One of the largest surviving gold caches of the Norsemen, unearthed at Hon in Norway, weighs just 5½ pounds. It in-

cludes coins mounted to make a necklace, and finger-rings.

Otherwise, Viking gold items tend to be recovered in groups of twos and threes. From Hornelund in Denmark, for example, come two splendid gold-filigree brooches, disk-shaped and intricately worked. Viking trading centers such as Hedeby in northern Germany and Birka in Sweden have also yielded some gold objects, as well as large quantities of non-precious, though beautiful, jewelry.

Perhaps the single most impressive golden relic of the Viking age was found at Tisso in Denmark in 1977 – again by a farmer. It is a massive neck-ring of intricately braided, pure gold strands. It weighs 4 pounds and is an incredible 14 inches in diameter.

ABOVE The stylized horse and bird on a gold Viking medallion were associated with the cult of Odin, the supreme creator god in Norse mythology.

RIGHT A hoard of Arab silver coins found in a 10th-century Viking grave in Sweden shows that the Norsemen's voyages in pursuit of booty or trade took them to the Middle East.

ABOVE The handle of a bucket from the Oseberg ship-burial in Norway is in the Celtic, rather than Viking, style. It was probably part of the loot from a Viking raid on Ireland in the 9th century AD.

A VIKING WAR CHEST

*I*n AD 865, Vikings from Denmark launched their biggest attack on England, with the aim not just of finding booty, but of settling there. By force of arms, they carved out a territory in the northern half of the country, the Danelaw, which was formally ceded to them by the English king Alfred in AD 886. The existence of the Danelaw, with its capital at York, bridged a gap in the Vikings' possessions, which now stretched unbroken from Dublin in Ireland across two seas to their Scandinavian homelands.

But the Vikings' occupation of parts of the British Isles was never entirely secure. There were revolts against their authority in Ireland, and in 910 the English began trying to wrest the Danelaw back. At some point in this troubled period, a Viking army from Ireland crossed into England with a hefty war chest. This was either hidden or lost in the English northeast, at Cuerdale in Lancashire.

The fighting fund was rediscovered in 1840, by workmen repairing the banks of the River Ribble. It is the biggest cache of Viking silver ever found anywhere, and weighs a hefty 88 pounds.

BELOW An ornate gold arm-ring from Jutland in Denmark carries tree-of-life symbols. In Norse mythology, the ash-tree Yggdrasil bound together heaven, earth, and hell.

By the 10th century, the Vikings had come to accept the uses of coinage, and the Cuerdale Hoard contains more than 7,000 silver coins. There are also silver ingots, and some intact items of jewelry, such as brooches or clasps used by the Norsemen to fasten their cloaks.

However, much of the silver jewelry has been cut into pieces. This is the so-called "hack silver" which the early Vikings favored instead of coins. Their wealth could be worn as ornamentation until the time came to spend some of it, when the necessary amount of precious metal could just be cut from a clasp, brooch, or armband with a sword.

ABOVE Gold, garnets, and niello (a black sulfur compound used for inlays) embellish a large silver-gilt buckle taken from a Viking chief's grave in Norway.

Hack silver turns up in many other Viking hoards. More than 1,000 silver caches have been found over the years in Scandinavia alone, for example at the trading center of Birka. But the haul from Cuerdale is four times heavier than the biggest of those.

King Alfred, who led English resistance against the Vikings, left treasure, too. In 1693, at Newton Park in Somerset, a gold-and-enamel enclosed jewel was found buried in a meadow known as the Field of Gold because of the number of gold coins retrieved there. The jewel, carved with the figure of a man, may once have been the head of a scepter or pointer. It dates from Alfred's epoch, and the gold surrounds bear a Saxon inscription which, translated, says: "Alfred caused me to be made."

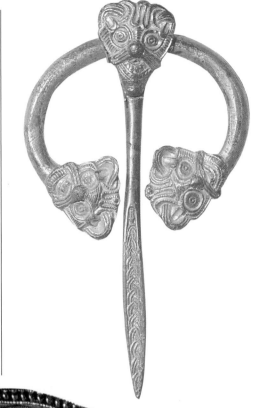

LEFT The Vikings used highly decorated, large-headed clasps or pins to fasten cloaks and dresses. This example, in bronze with gilding, is in the National Museum, Copenhagen.

LEFT A magnificent filigree gold disk brooch was originally set with five gems – rare for the Vikings, who preferred precious metal to jewels. It comes from the Hornelund hoard of Viking treasures, found in Denmark.

Fortunes of the Tsars

Ingenious, elaborate, painstakingly crafted from the most precious materials, excruciatingly expensive and above all quite without practical purpose or inspirational merit – the Easter "surprises" of Nicholas II, last Tsar of Russia, speak volumes about the man and his time, and about their maker, the court jeweler Pierre Fabergé.

Following a custom started by his predecessor Alexander III, Nicholas loved to give these costly baubles to his nearest and dearest. Fabergé's workshop loved making each of its "show-off" pieces more intricate than the next. A comparatively plain gold egg containing a brood of chicks yielded to a gold-and-enamel shell with a working model of a train inside. That in turn gave way to a diamond-encrusted gold offering with ivory miniatures of scenes from the Tsar's life or, in the same year of 1911, a golden-trunked bay tree, studded with rubies, pearls, and diamonds, on which a golden-feathered bird could be made to appear, sing, and disappear. Only about 36 of these surprises were made for the Russian royal family; today each is worth $2–4 million.

Rarely in modern times can so much money have been spent to such little point. So when Nicholas was forced to abdicate in 1917, imprisoned by the Bolsheviks and finally, according to the most widely accepted version of events, shot with his entire family in a Siberian basement in July 1918, rumors grew that the late Tsar must have had even more lavish treasures stashed safely somewhere.

They were largely misguided. The crown jewels and other panoply of Imperial Russia, or trinkets such as the Fabergé surprises, could not be spirited away. They were found and seized by the Bolsheviks, who sold some to help finance their revolution. The rest are now on display in Moscow's Kremlin and elsewhere. The Tsar's liquid assets in Russia, perhaps $5 million, were also expropriated. All Nicholas and his family took with them to their jail was personal jewelry, including such items as a platinum cross studded with diamonds, emeralds and pearls worn by the Tsarina Alexandra. Official reports say at least some of these were recovered shortly after the executions.

The rumors of treasure persisted, fed by the fact that the bodies of the Tsar and his wife were never found (although unsubstantiated, reports in 1988-89 claim

BELOW Pierre Fabergé (1846–1920) made only about three dozen of his multimillion dollar eggs for members of the Russian royal family, including the "Coronation Egg" of 1894. Others of his wealthy patrons commissioned similar baubles.

they now may have been). Nicholas was known to have had, at one time, huge deposits of cash and gold outside Russia; some money has been traced to a bank in Germany, but currency devaluations made it virtually worthless years ago. Stories that his gold still lies in the Bank of England have been consistently denied by bank officials.

Yet the tales of a hidden Tsarist treasure store are not entirely without foundation. Its track does not follow that of the ineffectual and ill-fated Nicholas, but those of his supporters who continued their struggle against the Bolshevik revolution for several years after 1918.

ABOVE Each delicately crafted Fabergé egg has its individual name. This one, with its portrait of Nicholas II and two of the royal children, is the "Lilies of the Valley Egg."

101

WHITE GOLD OF SIBERIA

The Bolshevik-led Russian revolution of November 1917 was not an overnight success. Bloody fighting between the Bolsheviks' Red Army and the White Army loyal to the former Tsar went on until 1920 according to Soviet histories, until 1922 in reality. The White forces started with the support of the big western powers. Two U.S. regiments, along with troops from Britain and a dozen other nations, fought and died on Russian soil, in an episode most but the Russians have long forgotten.

Supreme leader of the Whites from 1918 to 1920 was Admiral Alexander Kolchak, operating in the vast expanses of Siberia. In the south, around the Black Sea, the White forces were commanded by General Anton Denikin. Both needed huge war chests to keep the fight going, and both had them. Kolchak, nominally direct successor to the Tsar, reputedly amassed an incredible 500 tons of gold from the Imperial treasury and the donations of the aristocrats whose last hope to retain their power and privilege lay with the little Admiral. Kolchak's fund was smaller, but was said to include 450 pounds in platinum, baskets of gems, and millions of dollars' worth of gold rubles.

The fates of both massive fortunes are a mystery on which the veil has been lifted a tantalizing fraction. Recent developments in the Soviet Union may reveal more. After being within a whisker of complete victory

RIGHT The attack on the Winter Palace in what is now Leningrad was an early episode in the Bolshevik revolution of 1917. Tales abound of treasure lost in the turmoil of the revolution and the civil war that followed.

RIGHT Nicholas II guarded by Bolshevik soldiers during his captivity. Shortly after this photograph was taken, the Tsar and his family were shot in a Siberian basement.

ABOVE A poster proclaims the power of the Soviets, the revolutionary councils whose victorious Red Army eventually secured Russia for Lenin.

over the Reds, the White Army under Kolchak was in retreat by the end of 1919, forced back eastward along the route of the Trans-Siberian Railway with its treasure. But the Bolsheviks were a step ahead. They had seized the key city of Irkutsk, between the Whites and the Pacific. Kolchak had nowhere to go, surrendered, was tortured, and eventually shot. At that point, it seems reasonable to assume the Reds seized his war chest. But many accounts say the gold had disappeared before Kolchak threw in his hand, and the torture was intended to elicit its whereabouts.

In one version, it was hidden by the railroad west of Irkutsk, in a disused church or mine. The soldiers who had shifted it – all 500 tons – were then shot to preserve the secret. In another, the phenomenal hoard was offloaded just before Irkutsk and somehow manhandled onto the huge frozen expanse of Lake Baikal in an attempt to bypass the Bolshevik-held city and get it to safety further east. The gold, according to this story, had not cleared Baikal before the spring melt, and sank into the waters, the deepest of any lake in the world.

After Kolchak's death, Denikin, operating in the southwest theater of the war, took over nominal supreme command of the Whites, but he, too, was in retreat by 1920. His altogether more manageable treasure was moved out of Russia to Bulgaria, along the Black Sea coast, according to a book published in 1973. The author, Nicholas Svidine, claims to have been involved in burying it near Bourgas, and subsequently to have tried to retrieve it without success. Until recently, Bulgaria has had a hardline communist government, so Svidine's story could not be publicly tested. Perhaps soon it may be.

RIGHT Peasant soldiers of Kolchak's White Army in central Russia, 1919. A warchest consisting of 500 tons of gold is said to have gone missing when Kolchak was captured and killed.

A CONTINENT PILLAGED

BELOW Adolf Hitler, an unsuccessful painter himself, presided over the wholesale pillaging of art treasures throughout Europe. Unlike some of their earlier counterparts, though, Hitler's looters kept many masterpieces intact.

*I*n the entire history of warfare, no victors have looted conquered territory so systematically or on such a scale as the Nazis did in Europe and North Africa between 1938 and 1943. Even when the tide turned against them, the pillage continued under a momentum of its own. More than 40 years after the Nazis' final defeat, caches of their stolen treasures are still being found. Much will never be traced.

The sums involved cannot be calculated. Experts put the haul in bullion alone at an estimated $500 billion, of which about three-quarters is said to have been re-

covered. But this is based on official figures of shipments to Germany from banks and other institutions in the occupied countries. It does not take into account the valuables stripped, officially or in free-lance operations, from private individuals.

Nor does it include the artistic heritage of centuries torn from galleries, museums, and churches to make its way by the train-load to Germany for the greater glory of Hitler's Third Reich. Some of this booty was destined for a grandiose culture center in Hitler's home-city of Linz in Austria; under plans never put into action, the whole of Linz was to be turned into a vast living monument to Teutonic art and achievement.

When the U.S. 7th Army entered Neu-schwanstein Castle on the German-Austrian border in 1945, it found part of the ship-ments for Linz. Priceless paintings from all over occupied Europe had not even been taken out of their packing-cases – a story repeated countless times as other repositories were located.

As late as the 1980s, paintings stolen by the Nazis were still turning up. Some were found adorning the walls of a former Nazi living in quiet respectability in Holland. Bullion continues to appear, too. In 1983, in a monastery in northern Italy, chests containing 60 tons of gold and worth some $800 million at prevailing market prices were located, crammed into the shaft of an old well. The provenance of that parti-cular hoard could be traced back through Nazi records; it came in 1944 from the central bank in Rome, but appears to be only half of what was originally removed from the vaults. No one knows where the other half is now.

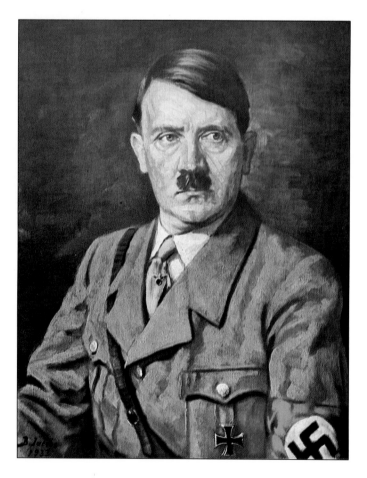

LE OPERE D'ARTE FIORENTINE TORNANO DALL'ALTO ADIGE ALLA LORO SEDE

Berlin, as the Reich capital, received a goodly share of looted treasures to add to those it already possessed. But in the confusion following the Allied victory in 1945, much disappeared from the city. One example of treasure which disappeared is the priceless collection of Mycenaean gold artifacts recovered by Heinrich Schliemann from the site of Troy in the 1870s (described in Chapter 2).

Rumors are prolific of unfound hoards of treasures concealed by Nazi leaders in the final days of the Second World War. Some are said to have reached bank vaults in Switzerland, South America, and Arab states, where they could still lie, protected by the rules of bank secrecy. Others reportedly underwent the traditional rites of treasure threatened in wartime – burial, concealment in caves or deep water.

ABOVE Trucks of the U.S. Fifth Army return art treasures stolen by the Nazis to the city of Florence in 1945. Caches of Nazi loot are still coming to light.

LAST DAYS OF DICTATORS

*D*epending on musical taste, the baroque splendors of Salzburg in Austria and the natural magnificence of the mountains around the city are forever associated with Wolfgang Amadeus Mozart, or *The Sound of Music*. But ancient Salzburg takes its name from the disused saltmines that burrow through the nearby hills. Somewhere in those, perhaps, or in a lake above, lies a massive hoard of treasure assembled by Adolf Hitler as his Nazis faced defeat in 1945.

Not far from Salzburg, high in the mountains, is the eagle's nest of Berchtesgaden, from where Hitler intended to mastermind the Nazis' last stand. As events happened, it never came – and stories persist in the locality of gold frenziedly hidden as Hitler's last supporters prepared their attempts to melt away.

The tales were fed by several bizarre incidents in the area during the 1950s. In one, a man was found in the mountains murdered by a bullet between the eyes. In another soon afterward, two climbers were stabbed to death; when their corpses were discovered, there were pits in the ground nearby, as though buried objects had been removed. Neither motives nor murderers have been traced in either case.

There have also been several attempts, in conditions of secrecy, to salvage items from mountain lakes above Salzburg. But the fate of Hitler's last war chest, if it existed at all, may never be revealed.

So far as is known, nothing has been found of treasure amassed by Field Marshal Erwin Rommel, one of Hitler's most brilliant commanders. In his North African campaign, successful at first, Rommel

MUSSOLINI'S TREASURE

By contrast, the whereabouts of treasure collected by another fascist dictator, Benito Mussolini, are in theory well known. Two huge suitcases of precious jewelry lie somewhere on the bottom of Lake Como in Italy, according to a member of Mussolini's German bodyguard, Captain Otto Kisnatt. By Kisnatt's own account, he threw them into the lake shortly after Mussolini and his mistress were captured and shot by Italian partisans in 1945. Kisnatt told his story to the Italian police in 1957, and a search of Lake Como was instituted. Nothing was found.

amassed large quantities of gold, jewelry, ivory, and works of art. Then, when the Allies recovered and moved toward their African victory, the loot was transferred to the Mediterranean island of Corsica. There, sometime in 1943, records of it petered out. According to one story, the treasure was taken to sea in a German ship and dumped overboard in the Gulf of Bastia, northeast of Corsica.

In the 1960s, a German ex-soldier appeared claiming to have taken part in this operation, and to know precisely where the booty lay, deep in 200 feet of water. He persuaded a group of American businessmen to finance a recovery attempt. Once the team was in the Gulf of Bastia, however, the veteran proved a disappointment. He could not, or would not, identify the spot. Subsequently, he disappeared.

Some contend that a powerful organization of ex-Nazis, depicted in Frederick

Forsyth's novel *The Odessa File*, had records of where their wartime colleagues hid loot, and quietly recovered what they could. Odessa, it is said, may have been responsible for the Salzburg slayings, and for the sudden silence of the informant about Rommel's treasure.

PRINCE CHARLIE'S CACHE

LEFT The wild charge of Prince Charlie's Highlanders overwhelmed the English at Prestonpans in 1745. But at Culloden, seven months later, the English had developed counter-tactics. They lost only 76 men, to the Highlanders' 1,200.

Bleak Culloden Moor, near Inverness in Scotland, was the graveyard of hope for Prince Charles Edward Stuart, the handsome young pretender to the throne of Britain. There, on April 16, 1746, his army of rebel Highlanders was crushed by the troops of the Hanoverian King George II. Bonnie Prince Charlie himself was forced to flee, to begin a desperate game of hide-and-seek with his enemies among the Scottish hills and islands.

King George's men put a price of £30,000 (perhaps $1 million today) on the fugitive's head. Despite that, no one betrayed him, and for five months he eluded his pursuers before taking ship to safety in France.

He was never to return. But in the early summer of 1746, Prince Charlie still believed he had lost only a battle, not the war. His army had at one stage come within 130 miles of London. His followers had proved their bravery and loyalty. He had powerful supporters across the water in France.

So plans were being laid for another uprising to reclaim for the Stuart dynasty the British crown it had once worn. The arrival on the Scottish west coast of French ships bearing some 35,000 gold pieces to finance the struggle was timely indeed.

Even while this war chest was being moved inland, the prince's men sighted government patrols. Hastily, the gold was divided into two hoards and buried. When the immediate danger was past, it was retrieved, and some of it used to pay Prince Charlie's followers. The rest – still a substantial sum – was put into six casks and buried again, this time more carefully.

Most of it was not reclaimed. When the prince finally gave up his fight and went to France on September 19, 1746, the secret of his war chest went with him. The casks are thought to be hidden somewhere around the shores of Loch Morar and Loch Arkaig, inland from the Scottish west coast port of Mallaig. Certainly, at one point in its travels, the money reached the grounds of Archancarry House, at the eastern end of Loch Arkaig.

King George's men, who conducted a reign of terror against the Scottish clans after Culloden, made their own, unsuccessful, attempts to find Prince Charlie's treasure. But any Highlanders who knew its precise whereabouts kept quiet, and when the search got too close, dozens of empty casks were scattered in the area to confuse the seekers.

RIGHT While evading King George's troops, Bonnie Prince Charlie crossed to the Isle of Skye disguised as "Betty Bourke," the maidservant of one of his supporters, Flora Macdonald. But with a price on his head, he could stay nowhere long – and, back in male dress, he bade Flora goodbye at the inne at Portree. His luggage consisted of a parcel containing four clean shirts, a cold fowl tied in a handkerchief, a bottle of brandy, and a bottle of whisky. He wore a new pair of shoes given to him by Sir Alexander Macdonald of Kingsburgh; Macdonald kept the old pair and after Macdonald's death they were bought by a Jacobite for £20 – a fortune in the 18th century.

6: RUMOR AND ROMANCE

Almost every country in the world has its local tales of treasure lost or hidden, but not yet found. Some are based on undisputed historical fact, some lean heavily toward legend. The United States is no exception to both categories.

The authentic is supplied, for example, by the wreck-raising activities of people such as Kip Wagner and Mel Fisher.

The romantic rumors are legion, from the pirate gold of Blackbeard and Lafitte, to the Lost Dutchman and other missing mines. Many have at least a basis in truth, and we look at some of those here.

Sadly, there is a third category – the outright lie dreamed up by the unscrupulous to fleece the unwary. No certainties exist in treasure tracking. The grizzled old man selling the battered map, or the box-numbered ad for a mysterious code, could just be for real. If so, though, the question must be: Why share the secret of a long-lost fortune with total strangers?

BLACKBEARD'S HELLISH PIT

ABOVE Edward "Blackbeard" Teach hid his pirate treasure in an underground cave where, he boasted, only he and the Devil could find it. The hoard has never been traced.

Virgin Islands and New Providence Island in the Bahamas. But his raids on merchantmen took him as far north at least as Virginia in 1716-18, and among his favorite hunting grounds were the waters of the Carolinas. It is said that Blackbeard had struck a secret deal with Governor Charles Eden of North Carolina to help him dispose of booty.

Even his bloodthirsty fellow pirate captains had no cause to love Teach. He boasted to them of a vast treasure-store in a pit or underground vault "where none but Satan and myself can find it." Blackbeard did not just keep treasure there. According to stories that smack perhaps too much of another similarly named villain, the Bluebeard of play and opera,

BELOW Pirate dramas enthralled audiences in the 18th and 19th centuries, though they bore little resemblance to reality. A Mr. Helme played Blackbeard in 1799.

O f all the pirates to operate off the American coast in the 18th century, none was more fearsome looking than saturnine, staring-eyed Edward Teach. The bushy black beard that gave him his nickname was spiked with lighted tapers during his raids, to strike further terror into his victims.

At various times in his infamous career, Blackbeard had bases at St. Thomas in the

Mʳ HELME as BLACKBEARD the PIRATE.
As Performed at the Royal Circus, Feb. 10ᵗʰ 1799.

Teach walled up in the vault women companions of whom he grew tired, leaving them to die while looking at his wealth.

The boasting and the cruelty were fairly normal for the time and place. But Blackbeard offended his pirate colleagues by stealing from them, too. On one occasion, he put men aboard a ship belonging to Stede Bonnet to help quell a mutiny, and then stripped it of all the booty he found there. Bonnet, a Barbados landowner who allegedly turned to piracy because of a nagging wife, was no saint himself. He was one of the few pirates who actually did make his victims walk the plank, and was hanged for this and general crimes in Charleston in 1718. Nevertheless, Blackbeard's demonstration that there is no honor among thieves incensed him, and Bonnet spent the rest of his life out for revenge.

Bonnet's haul presumably joined the rest in Blackbeard's underground hideaway. The whereabouts of that went with Blackbeard to his grave, when the fearsome freebooter was finally killed by Lieutenant Rob Maynard, in an encounter with the British Navy near the Outer Banks, North Carolina.

So far as is known, no one has yet become the third party to Blackbeard's shared secret with the devil, and found the treasure-store. Some believe it could be the "money pit" on Oak Island, Nova Scotia, described in Chapter 1, which has defied all attempts to resolve its mysteries since 1795. The dates associated with Oak Island fit Blackbeard slightly better than they do William Kidd, whose name is often linked to the money pit. But there is no evidence that Blackbeard ranged as far north as Nova Scotia.

ABOVE The islands of the Bahamas were one of the refuges used by Blackbeard, but he foraged far to the north in search of merchant ships to plunder.

THE BROTHERS LAFITTE

By the beginning of the 19th century, old-style buccaneering was on its last legs in the Caribbean, the Gulf of Mexico, and surrounding waters. Spain's empire of the Americas was crumbling. Spanish shipments of treasure back to Europe, which had once drawn freeboot-

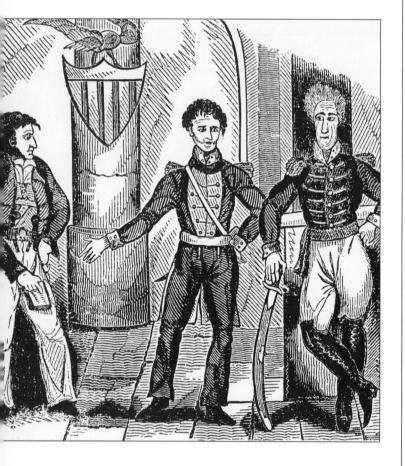

ABOVE Spurning the overtures of the British, Jean Lafitte (left) offers his services to Governor Claiborne and General Andrew Jackson before the Battle of New Orleans.

ing raiders by the hundred, were more or less at an end. The navies of Britain, France, and the United States were committed to stamping out the remnants of piracy.

Yet some nests of pirates lingered on in the area. One of them was in Barataria Bay on the humid Louisiana coast, where a buccaneer known as Grambo held sway.

Into this hotbed of crime, in 1809, came the Lafitte brothers – Pierre and Jean. The pair were blacksmiths by trade, but had opted for the easier, and far better-paying, life of plunderers.

In 1811, Jean seized command of the pirate colony, shooting Grambo. With military skill, he fortified the refuge, mounting stolen cannons to guard the narrow channel leading to Barataria between the islands of Grande Terre and Grande Ile. From this protected hideaway, the pirates foraged under Jean's command, with any passing ship as fair game and lucrative sidelines in smuggling and slave-running. For relaxation, the pirates repaired to the fleshpots of New Orleans.

Over the following two years, the Lafittes and their men grew richer and more un-scrupulous. The Governor of Louisiana publicly denounced them for piracy, but they ignored the warning, and eventually the Lafittes were indicted and arrested. Lavish spreading of their wealth ensured they were acquitted at their trial.

By this time, in 1814, the U.S. was at war with Britain. The British, knowing Jean's skill and daring, as well as his lack of love for the U.S. authorities, offered him a naval commission and a large pay-ment to fight for them. Instead, he chose the American side, assisting General Andrew Jackson to win the Battle of New Orleans. In return, both Lafittes received free pardons for their previous crimes.

Jean obviously did not consider that reward enough. Shortly afterward, he went back to piracy. Barataria was no longer safe, and he moved his base of operations along the coast to the islands of Texas, but that was flushed out by the

LEFT A highly romantic portrait of Jean Lafitte, one of the last and best-known of U.S. pirates. Some say his treasure still lies in a Louisiana bayou.

U.S. Navy in 1826. Jean then disappeared, and with him the fortune he was supposed to have amassed. According to one account, he was killed a couple of years later in a skirmish with a British ship. More popularly, he is said to have adopted a new identity as a prosperous merchant, and kept up this incognito until his death in 1854.

To this day, there are those in Louisiana who swear that Jean Lafitte left a vast store of plunder hidden somewhere in the bayous he knew so well, to reclaim when the heat died down. It has to be said, though, the evidence is against it. Much of what he accumulated he spent, and some at least was recovered by the Louisiana authorities.

THE GOLD RUSH IS ON!

ABOVE A Californian gold nugget reproduced life-size in Britain's The Illustrated London News, *January 1850. Articles like this brought prospectors flooding to the Golden State from all over the world, but few struck lucky.*

The waves of gold fever that periodically swept the United States in the 19th century literally moved nations and mountains. Tens of thousands of fortune-hunters from all over the world scrambled to the site of the latest strike, to pan, cradle, tunnel, or blast for their share of the precious metal. The mass migrations inevitably brought the prospectors into conflict with the Indians whose lands they wanted to cross or to work. Many hopefuls died at Indian hands, but eventually and inevitably the Indians were driven from their ancestral hunting grounds.

A pattern was set at the tail end of the Appalachians in northeast Georgia. It was Cherokee territory when the nation's first gold rush hit it in 1829, and the Cherokees refused to sell. Within a year, the State of Georgia had assumed ownership. Within three more, the region had been organized administratively. At its heart was Dahlonega, seat of Lumpkin County and site of a branch of the U.S. mint that coined more than $6 million from Georgia gold in 1838-61.

It was the same in Alaska in 1880, when gold was discovered near present-day Juneau, and in 1896-98, when it was found in the Klondike and at Anvil Creek near Nome. At Skagway, base for the Klondike rush, there was only one log cabin before 20,000 prospectors descended on the area. Around Nome, a 15-mile-long city of tents sprang up on the beaches to accommodate 12,000 fortune hunters.

With all these people milling around, there was precious little chance much gold would go unnoticed, or that any prospector could strike lucky and keep it secret for

SUTTER'S MILL GOLD

On January 24, 1848, James Wilson Marshall saw glittering particles in the tail-race of Sutter's Mill. His exclamation "Boys, I think I have found a gold mine" unwittingly precipitated the California gold rush of 1848-49, which eventually yielded upward of $1 billion in precious metal. Though Marshall and Sutter tried to keep the find secret at first, it soon leaked out. A vanguard of perhaps 80,000 people stampeded to the Golden State; within four years, the white population of California had increased more than tenfold.

Mill-owner John Sutter.

Gold-finder James Marshall.

Sutter's Mill, where the '49 rush began.

long. In California and western Nevada, particularly, there are tales still told of lost mines and hidden caches around such places as Auburn and the "ghost town" of Bodie, where the mines once yielded $400,000 in bullion a month. Mostly, they are just tales.

Many of those Forty-Niners who hit pay dirt spent it fast and furiously in the saloons and gambling dens of towns like Bodie or on the coast in San Francisco. A few handled it more wisely – though not always luckily. Dozens of successful fortune-hunters tried to take their treasure home but were lost with their valuables aboard the paddle-steamer *SS Central America* which foundered off South Carolina in 1857 and is now being salvaged. In a similar incident, another paddle-steamer, the *Golden Gate*, sank near Manzanillo in Mexico in 1862, reputedly carrying California gold and coin to the then value of $1,600,000, which is not thought to have been recovered.

Some of the unlucky Forty-Niners gave up on California and began to seek their

LEFT From New York to San Francisco by sea took three months in 1849. For those who could afford it, the ocean route to the goldfields was probably safer than overland.

fortunes further inland, in the arid lands of Arizona and New Mexico. There, they were less under the prying eyes of rivals, but more at risk from the Indians whose land they threatened.

LEFT Prospectors at work in the Sierras. Cradles, which were rocked and flushed through with water, were a less strenuous way than traditional panning for extracting gold from "pay dirt."

GOLD OF THE THUNDER GOD

*W*hen thunder rolls around the dust-dry cliffs and canyons of Arizona's Superstition Mountain, locals claim they hear in it a cruel and ghostly laugh. Somewhere amid the high peaks, they say, the shade of long-dead Jacob Walz is again mocking those who seek his golden lode – the United States' most notorious hidden treasure, the Lost Dutchman Mine.

In this harsh, rattlesnake-infested wilderness east of Phoenix, it is not hard to believe in ghosts. For centuries, Superstition

BELOW Frederic Remington, one of the best-loved illustrators of the Old West, called this picture "The Gold Bug." Pack-mules or burros were far better suited than horses to the harsh terrain where gold was found.

THE 'OLD DUTCHMAN'

A far bigger prize – the source of the gold itself, the Peraltas' mine remained to be found. Almost from the time of the slaughter, fortune hunters began to look for it; some reputedly found it, but were murdered or otherwise died before they could benefit. One finder who did live to profit, according to legend at least, was the man for whom the mine is now named the "Old Dutchman" Jacob Walz.

Actually a German, Walz is said to have learned the whereabouts of the mine either from a member of the Peralta family, or from an Apache woman who was Walz's mistress. For more than 20 years until his death in 1891, he paid mysterious visits to Superstition Mountain, returning with gold worth upward of $300,000 in all. On his deathbed, he left the tantalizing clues to the mine's location that tourists and treasure seekers try to follow today.

Mountain was sacred to the Apaches, the home of their thunder god. Here, in the 16th century, Spanish conquistadors came in search of gold and silver, many to die at the hands of the Indians or from the countless natural hazards of the terrain.

Here, too, the wealthy and powerful Peralta family, descendants of the conquistadors, came in 1845. They found gold, in huge quantities, somewhere near the peak that they named Sombrero and today is Weaver's Needle. They left a legacy of greed and hate which, over a century and a half, has littered the cliffs and canyons

with the bodies of the dead.

The Peraltas and their men mined the Superstition Mountain gold for several years, partially refining it on site and shipping out millions of dollars' worth. But the Apaches were watching this intrusion on sacred ground. In 1848, they prepared to strike back.

Somehow, the Peraltas learned of the Apache plan. The mine entrance was hastily concealed, and the partially refined gold was loaded onto every available burro. Some stories say there was too much gold to transport, and a portion was buried near the mine. In any case, it availed the Peraltas nothing. As the laden train moved out toward the town of Sonora and safety, the Apaches attacked, slaughtering all the miners at the place now called Massacre Ground, and scattering the terrified gold-bearing burros to the four winds.

For years after the carnage, prospectors on Superstition Mountain were still recovering saddlebags full of gold from the spots where the burros eventually died or shucked their loads. The most recent reported find was in 1914, and it is generally thought there are no more to trace.

ABOVE In search of gold – a group of prospectors in the 19th-century West. Jacob Walz, founder of a U.S. legend, was apparently more successful than most prospectors.

THE LOST DUTCHMAN

RIGHT Revolvers and rifles were essential to prospectors in Arizona in Jacob Walz's day, to shoot wild animals – or claim-jumpers. Walz reputedly killed several men to protect the secret of the Lost Dutchman mine.

he mine can be found at the spot on which the shadow of the tip of Weaver's Needle rests at four in the afternoon," Jacob Walz is supposed to have declared just before he died in 1891. The curmudgeonly "Old Dutchman" – a self-confessed murderer and suspected gold-thief – added other details to indicate that the mine is in or near a canyon, facing west, and about a mile away from an otherwise unspecified cave. In the wasteland of Superstition Mountain, the instructions turn out to be vague, like much about Walz himself.

Even Walz's real name is uncertain; it is sometimes spelt Waltz, or given as Von Walzer. Trained in Germany as a mining engineer, he turned up in the United States during the Californian gold rush of 1848-49, working in various mines in California and Arizona before appearing in the area of Superstition Mountain around 1870. In his early days in Arizona, Walz is said to have stolen gold from one of his employers, though that was never proved.

His first trip to Superstition Mountain is thought to have been in 1871, possibly with a member of the Peralta family who then disappeared from the scene. At any rate, by 1879 Walz was back in the canyons with a partner, fellow-German Jacob Weiser. They were eventful forays. On one, the pair allegedly discovered and killed two Mexicans working the mine, before returning to Phoenix with gold. On another, Weiser was attacked by Apaches, receiving wounds from which he eventually died. Walz escaped unharmed.

By this time, Walz had become a notorious figure in Phoenix. Drunken and hot-tempered, he was followed everywhere by people anxious to learn the mine's whereabouts, and his journeys to Superstition became less frequent and more clandestine. Even so, he periodically brought back more gold. With Weiser gone, he seems to have considered his nephew Julius as a new partner, only to think again and kill the youngster to keep his secret – the murder to which he confessed as he lay dying. Walz is also a suspect in the deaths of two former soldiers, found killed on the route to Superstition after they had boasted of a gold strike there.

In 1890, Walz made his last trip to the mountain, retrieving a small amount of gold. By the following year, he was dead.

Those who knew of the Old Dutchman's directions to his mine included Dick Holmes and Reinhart Petrash. They spent years looking for the site without success. Others had better luck.

At the turn of the century, a Denver man called Charles Hall found gold, not under Weaver's Needle as Walz's clues suggested, but close to where the Apaches had slaughtered the men from the original Peralta mine. A boom town grew up around Hall's lode, from which several million dollars' worth of precious metal was extracted until the whole site was destroyed in a landslide brought on by torrential rain, and abandoned. At least two later attempts have been made to re-open the workings, but the position of the lode in relation to the surface has shifted, and the main gold vein has not been retraced.

There are plenty who believe, with some reason, that this site cannot be the source of Walz's wealth, and continue to look elsewhere. One was Adolph Ruth of Washington, who arrived at Superstition in 1931 with what he was convinced was a map pinpointing the mine. His remains were found months later. He had been shot and decapitated, and the map had gone. Others to die in the gold quest include Stanley Fernandez, murdered by his partner Benjamin Ferreira in 1959 after a quarrel. But none of this history of bloodshed deters the treasure hunters who still flock to Superstition.

LEFT Even in the age of the auto, the Apache country of Arizona can be forbidding. Somewhere in the dry canyons of Superstition Mountain a fortune in gold could still be waiting . . .

LOST HOARD OF THE BIG HORN

The Bozeman Trail linking the goldfields of Montana to the east was no place for the fainthearted in 1876. Just a few years earlier, the Sioux Indians under Red Cloud had massacred an 80-strong cavalry troop and burned down Fort Phil Kearny, built to protect travelers using the trail. Now the Sioux had taken up arms again, in a combined force with the Cheyenne and led by chiefs Sitting Bull and Crazy Horse.

Among those charged with putting down the rising and driving the tribes back to their reservations was Lieutenant Colonel George Custer. He was an unfortunate choice in several respects. A headstrong glory hunter, he had also unloosed a gold-rush in the Black Hills of Dakota by reporting gold there "from the grassroots down," after a scouting expedition in 1874. The site was sacred to the Sioux, and clashes between them and fevered prospectors heading for the Black Hills contributed to the unrest of 1876.

Custer's lack of judgment was to lead him into the Battle of the Little Big Horn, where he and his command of more than 200 men were wiped out by an overwhelmingly larger Indian force on June 25, 1876.

Gil Longworth, driving a wagon laden with gold from the Montana fields east along the Bozeman Trail that same June, knew nothing of Custer's fateful activities some 40 miles or more away to the south-east. Longworth did know he himself was in imminent peril from the Sioux. So, according to the American writer E.C. Schumacher, when he encountered a U.S. Cavalry supply boat on the Big Horn River, he pleaded to be allowed to load the gold aboard. The captain, Grant Marsh, agreed. Longworth would not abandon the wagon and left with it. Much later, his mangled body was found.

Marsh, meanwhile, began to regret his offer of assistance. From the riverboat moored in midstream, he became more and more aware of hostility around him. Perhaps to give the boat a better turn of speed should the need arise, he and two companions rowed the gold to the west bank of the Big Horn and buried it there.

The riverboat captain could not return to recover it. A U.S. Cavalry force under Brigadier General Alfred Terry had engaged the Sioux and put them to flight, and Marsh's boat was needed to ferry the wounded toward safety.

Following the death of Custer, public opinion was incensed against the Indians, and efforts to subdue them were intensified. In that climate, it was not possible to reclaim the buried gold quickly, but in 1879 Marsh apparently tried to trace its rightful owners, without success.

There is no evidence that he dug it up for himself, and it may still be somewhere along the course of the Big Horn – at today's prices worth perhaps $1 million.

LEFT George Armstrong Custer (1839–76) inspired a Dakota gold-rush that angered the Sioux. As Custer died at the Little Big Horn, a gold consignment went missing.

THE BEALE CODE

For more than 100 years, U.S. treasure seekers have been frustrated by a complex numerical coded message that, if cracked, promises to lead to an underground cache containing 2,921 pounds of gold, 5,100 pounds of silver, and a fortune in jewelry, near Montvale in Bedford County, Virginia. Even modern computers have so far failed to penetrate the ciphers and reveal the precise location of the hoard.

Our knowledge of the code, and of the circumstances under which it was purport-edly drawn up, come entirely from a pamphlet published in 1885 by James B. Ward of Virginia. But the story begins nearly seven decades earlier, in 1817.

That year, one Thomas Jefferson Beale, a tall and handsome adventurer, is said to have led a 30-strong hunting expedition from Virginia to the western plains, during which members of the party discovered rich veins of gold and silver in a ravine 300 miles or so north of Santa Fe. Beale and his companions extracted the precious metals and, between 1819 and 1821, laboriously transported them back East. Some of the silver was exchanged in St. Louis for jewelry, and that, with the rest of the silver and the huge quantity of gold, was hidden in a stone-lined vault dug for the purpose in Bedford County, about 4 miles from a tavern known as Buford's.

By 1822, Beale is said to have been stay-ing in Lynchburg, planning another hunt-ing expedition to the West. Fearing that he might not return, he left at his hotel a locked box which he asked the hotel-keeper, Robert Morriss, to look after for him. Later, from St. Louis, Beale sent Morriss a letter instructing him to open the box if no one had reclaimed it within ten years, and adding that a key would be forwarded to him by a third party in 1832. Beale then disappeared, never to be heard of again.

The 1832 deadline came and went, with no word to Morriss from anyone and no sign of a key. The hotelkeeper is said to have waited another 13 years before finally forcing the lock and revealing the contents of the box – two letters from Beale, several other notes that Morriss dismissed as un-important, and three sets of figures. One

THE BEALE CIPHERS

of the letters told Morriss of the existence of the treasure hoard, asked him to superintend its distribution to the original members of the hunting party or their beneficiaries, and explained that the figures were a code revealing the location of

key text, the pattern seems random.

According to his pamphlet, Ward struggled on for years, until he finally linked one section of the coded message to the Declaration of Independence. That told him how much gold and silver was in the

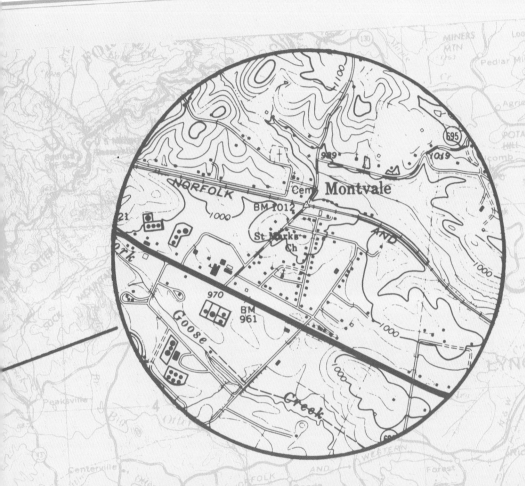

the vault, its contents, and the names and addresses of those who were to share in the booty. An explanation of the code itself was promised to Morriss "in time." Like the key to the box, it never arrived.

Morriss apparently made no progress in cracking the code and, shortly before he died in 1863, he handed the letters and ciphers to Ward, the son of a friend. By his own account, Ward swiftly recognized that the figures are a key code, in which each number represents a letter in a given written text – for example, a passage from the Bible. But unless the text can be identified, such codes are very hard to decipher. Many different numbers represent just one letter, according to the way that the letter is distributed in the key text. Without the

vault, and that it was in Bedford County. But beyond that, it did not help. Other written texts had evidently been used for the other two sets of figures – and despite renewed efforts, Ward could not work out what they were. Eventually, worn out and broke, Ward published all the information he had, in the hope that he might obtain at least some recompense for his trouble.

Or so he claimed. Believers in the authenticity of the code insist that Beale, Morriss, and Ward all showed themselves too serious-minded to perpetrate a hoax. But one of the most infamous hoaxes in the history of British archaeology – Piltdown Man – was the product of a serious mind. Until the Beale Code is finally deciphered, no one can be sure.

I N D E X

P I C T U R E   C R E D I T S

The Publishers would like to thank the following for providing pictures for this book:

The Beale Cypher Association: pages 124/125.
Christie's Colour Library: pages 3, 46 and 47.
CM Dixon: pages 53 (bottom), 54, 55 (middle and bottom), 57 (right), 64 (bottom), 67 (top and middle), 70/71, 72 (background), 74 (left), 80, 81, 82, 83, 84 (right), 85, 89, 92, 93, 94, 95, 96, 97, 98 and 99.
ET Archive: pages 10, 11 (top), 56, 87, 88 and 108.
Mary Evans Picture Library: pages 15 (bottom), 17 (top), 18, 26, 27, 33, 49 (top), 57 (left, top and bottom), 61, 103 (top right and bottom), 109 and 123.
The FORBES Magazine Collection, New York: pages 100 (© H Peter Curran) and 101 (© Larry Stein).
By courtesy of the Italian State Tourist Office (E.N.I.T.) London: pages 90/91 and 107 (top).
GeoScience Features Picture Library: pages 25 (main picture), 50/51, 62, 63, 64 (top), 65, 67 (bottom), 68 (bottom) and 69.
Greater Miami Convention & Visitors' Bureau: page 38 and back jacket.
The Illustrated London News Picture Library: pages 23 (top right and bottom), 25 (inset), 48, and 84 (left).
The MacQuitty International Photographic Collection: pages 73, 74 (right), 75, 76, 77, 78 and 79.
The Mansell Collection: pages 17 (bottom), 37 (top right), 43 (top), 52, 53 (top and bottom right), 58, 59, 68 (top), 72 (insets), 102 and 112 (left).
Peter Newark's American Collection: pages 66 and 155.
Peter Newark's Historical Pictures: pages 11 (bottom), 12 (left), 14, 15 (top), 16, 19, 22, 23 (top left), 37 (top left), 39, 42, 43 (bottom), 112 (right) and 114.
Peter Newark's Military Pictures: pages 49 (middle and bottom), 103 (top left), 104, 105, 106 and 107 (bottom).
Peter Newark's Western Americana: pages 1, 8/9, 13 (top), 110/111, 113, 116, 117, 118, 119, 120 and 121.
Nova Scotia Information Service: pages 20 and 21.
Planet Earth Pictures:
  © Mike Ross: page 44 (bottom);
  © Flip Schulke: pages 12 (right), 13 (bottom), 32, 40 and 45;
  © Flip & Debra Schulke: page 41;
  © Warren Williams: pages 30/31, 31 and 37 (main picture).
Guy Ryecart: front jacket.
Iles of Scilly Museum Association/Philip Michell: page 44 (top).
Mick Sharp: © Dave Longley: page 55 (top).
Vasamuseet (The Vasa Museum), Stockholm: pages 34 and 35.
Peter Vine: pages 6/7, 28 and 29.